# Reflective Discipline

# Reflective Discipline

## *Reducing Racial Disparity in Referrals and Suspensions*

Martha R. Bireda

ROWMAN & LITTLEFIELD
Lanham • Boulder • New York • London

Published by Rowman & Littlefield
An imprint of The Rowman & Littlefield Publishing Group, Inc.
4501 Forbes Boulevard, Suite 200, Lanham, Maryland 20706
www.rowman.com

6 Tinworth Street, London SE11 5AL

British Library Cataloguing in Publication Information Available

**Library of Congress Cataloging-in-Publication Data**

ISBN 978-1-4758-4902-8 (cloth)
ISBN 978-1-4758-4903-5 (pbk)
ISBN 978-1-4758-4904-2 (electronic)

Dedicated to African American students;
May your path to a successful future
Be cleared by teachers and administrators,
Who see you through a new lens,
Free of historical stereotypes.

# Contents

# Foreword

It is an honor to write the foreword for the third edition of Dr. Bireda's work related to racial disparity in discipline. Dr. Bireda's previous books have addressed the need for cultural sensitivity in the classroom.

The importance of cultural reinforcements within the classroom has long been established. Research demonstrates a correlation between the two as well as indicators of the failures as a result of the lack thereof. Since that time, it is painfully clear that this research has not developed into nationwide cognitive pedagogical strategies, and we need these tactics to provide the best learning environments for all children. What we are witnessing are failures of an unimaginable degree.

Disciplinary action has become the tool for teachers to rid themselves of challenging students. What these students need is the understanding of their culture by educators. Closing the cultural disconnect opens the communication gap that right now kills learning. The counterproductive policies within today's classroom and school settings create an inability to relate, student low self-esteem, truancy, misbehavior, and eventual dropping out that leads to incarceration. Today's tactics prevent understanding that leads to an atmosphere that fosters learning.

Educational policies now simply make it easier to send referrals that will rid teachers of the problem rather than helping them discover various multicultural pedagogical strategies to resolve the student's learning issue. The process of pushing minority students out through disciplinary measures does not deal with fundamental issues and root causes. It is no way to solve the levels of school violence, classroom disruption, and the complete disservice done to minority students across the country because their mandatory education does not relate to them, takes advantage of them, and prevents them from learning.

To rectify the situation, we must begin to balance these theoretical aspects of pedagogical issues pertaining to cultural reinforcements with historical issues that deal with current conditions.

This book is a good step in that direction. It examines school discipline of minority students and the need to work within to create sustainable curriculum and discipline policy changes that reinforce students' culture instead of their resentment. Current minority disciplinary statistics create a horrific disconnect between the teacher and student that alters the ability to learn, advance, and become contributing citizens. This book presents a practical guide for immediate resolution that is a sound framework for a solid future of educated minorities that will advance their lives and the country's well-being.

# Acknowledgments

A very special thanks to:

Dr. Tom Koerner, who suggested that it was time for a third edition of this book that answers the "why" of the persistent racial disparity in discipline.

Dr. Michael Desjardins, who shared information about the classification of subjective student offenses.

Libraries are essential to researchers and writers. I so appreciate the endless patience, desire, and ability to locate interlibrary loans for me by Jessica Crimaudo and the smiling face of LeAnn Beckwith each time a new book arrived. Both are great members of the Charlotte County Library System (Florida).

Manuscripts are just words on paper until an editor uses her special talents to create a book. Thank you so very much Colleen for your special attention to this book. You edited it with a sense of empathy, compassion, and truth that I so admire in you as an editor. You are truly a great writer as well, and I hope that soon we will be able to collaborate.

It is the students who have given truth and merit to each edition of this book. I appreciate the openness and honesty of the middle-school "high fliers" (students with repeated suspensions) that I worked with in the New Image Project. These young men learned as many strategies as possible for adolescents, so as to prevent their being entrapped in situations that would cause them to be suspended.

My thank-you to Mr. Derrick Middlebrooks and his students in the Scholars Club for allowing me to hear the stories of African American and Hispanic adolescents and their expectations for the future.

Those who are willing to read manuscripts are always necessary and appreciated. Thank you, Maureen Peters and Myrna Charry for reading the manuscript and for your helpful comments.

Thank you to Carlie Wall and Andrew Yoder for their commitment to discipline equity and to their professionalism in bringing this project to fruition.

A special thank-you to Dr. Anthony E. Dixon, author and history professor at Bethune-Cookman University, for his insightful foreword.

My children, Jaha and Saba, have always been my greatest supporters. Now both adults, I have fond memories of Jaha finding journals for me and Saba waiting with nickels in hand to make copies of articles. Finally, my new grandson, Nahom, has become a great inspiration for my work. His being in my life has deepened my commitment to do what is mine to do to ensure that all children attend schools where they are nurtured, encouraged, and emotionally secure.

# Introduction

Educators today have an incredibly difficult task. They work long hours without adequate pay or recognition for the job that they do. The majority are good teachers, administrators, and staff who wish to make a positive difference in the lives of all students.

We have come to a point, however, when we must acknowledge that many policies and actions related to discipline are negatively impacting a large percentage of our nation's school population, that of students of color, especially African American students.

Racial disparity in discipline is a form of institutional racism. It is unfortunate that in the institution that students must legally attend and that is meant to prepare them for life as contributing citizens, racism exists. For almost fifty years, since the desegregation of US schools, we have never confronted the root cause of racism in our schools; culturally conditioned beliefs informed by racist images that are deeply rooted in the American mind. Until we "see" African American students, especially males, differently, racism will persist in the public schools of the United States.

Although the first two editions of *Cultures in Conflict* (2002, 2009) dealt primarily with cultural issues, the persistence and severity of the problem of racism in our schools makes it crucial that we address race as the primary mission and cultural differences secondarily.

Focusing on racism in our schools is a difficult and controversial task, but the criminalization of African American students and the school-to-prison pipeline make this edition all the more essential.

The name of the third edition, *Reflective Discipline*, reflects our primary focus and approach. This current edition is written specifically as a guide to assist educators in changing the images that we hold of African American students, especially males. Unless we view these students differently, change our perceptions and assumptions about their intelligence, culture, and character, they face an institutional racism that denies them equal educational opportunity and life chances.

Since the second edition of *Cultures in Conflict: Eliminating Racial Profiling* was published in 2010, the racial dynamics in schools have worsened. The situation has become more crucial as schools have become more hostile to students of color, especially African American students. These students now face forms of racism that have more destructive consequences for them than ever before.

Zero-tolerance policies, pervasive in schools serving predominately low-income African American students, and police in schools has led to the criminalization of African American students, which has culminated in the school-to-prison-pipeline. Racism in education, the institution responsible for preparing our youth for adulthood and citizenship, must aggressively address the endemic racism in education.

This third edition; *Reflective Discipline* is a direct appeal to the moral integrity, ethics, and professionalism of educators, "to see African American and other students of color differently." The most recent research indicates that "implicit bias," informed by racist stereotypes culturally conditioned in US society influences racial disparities in disciplinary policies, referrals, and actions.

As educators, we must examine our beliefs, expectations, and behaviors as they relate to students of color, particularly African American students. This third edition provides an awareness of how these racial stereotypes became so ingrained in our culture by examining our personal beliefs, expectations, and behaviors influenced by this cultural conditioning. These culturally conditioned beliefs and assumptions about African American students have a tremendous impact on teacher–student rapport and relationships.

The primary focus of the updated edition of this book will continue to be African American students. Recent studies indicate that African American females face the same disparities in discipline as African American males. Both groups are now the most likely to be disproportionately represented in disciplinary referrals, suspensions, and expulsions.

This edition will continue to provide administrators, teachers, and auxiliary staff (i.e., school resource officers [SROs]) with a knowledge base related to the culture of African American students. Specifically, the reader will gain an awareness of the culturally influenced communication style of African American students that often contributes to tension in classroom interactions with their teachers.

A majority of teachers are white and female; this book can be of particular assistance in helping them to better understand the culturally based and culturally conditioned factors that influence disciplinary incidents involving African American students. This book will also be beneficial to all teachers who desire to better understand how the social class of the teacher and student has an influence on the student–teacher interaction and disciplinary incidents.

The new phenomenon of "adultification," the unique developmental tasks of African American students, but also the way in which racism influences the fears and anxieties they face in both the society at large and in the school environment is necessary to include in the third edition. Adultification and its impact as a precipitating factor that increases the potential for African American students to be referred for disciplinary actions will be examined.

The most significant concept introduced in the third edition is the concept of "Reflective Discipline." Reflective Discipline asks the "why" of student misbehavior free of culturally conditioned stereotypes and uses an educational approach to correct misbehavior. This third edition is structured in such a way that it might be used for an administrator/faculty/staff book study or implemented as an in-service workshop.

This book provides questions, exercises, and activities designed to generate reflection among individuals and groups related to race and disciplinary issues. This book provides a blueprint for educators to make the crucial changes that will reduce racially disproportionate referrals and actions and to see African American students differently.

As educators, our goal is that American education be exceptional, inclusive, and highly regarded in the global context. In societies like Finland, which has a world-renowned educational system, educators believe that every child is valuable and that no child can fall through the cracks; the stability and economic welfare of their nation depends upon all children reaching that same level of exceptionality.

Part I, chapter 1, includes an overview of the most current research data related to racial disproportionality in discipline. Chapter 2 deals with persistent factors (i.e., zero tolerance) and high-stakes testing that have influenced disproportionality in discipline.

Chapter 3 addresses new threats that promote racialized discipline practices in our schools. The focus is the new form of stereotyping of African American students, adultification (i.e., policing in the school environment and the crucial training needed by the SROs to prevent the criminalization of African American students).

In chapter 4, the concept of Reflective Discipline is introduced.

In part II, chapter 5, the source, purpose, perpetuation, and reinforcement of culturally conditioned beliefs based on racist ideology is explored in detail.

In chapter 6, the impact of culturally conditioned beliefs and images in the classroom is examined.

Chapter 7 addresses the influence of cultural differences on classroom interactions between African American students and teachers.

In chapter 8, the impact of the lack of cultural knowledge and insensitivity is described.

Chapter 9 describes normal adolescent development and challenges and the unique developmental tasks faced by African American youth.

Part IV addresses the school culture and climate.

Chapter 10 focuses on racism in the school environment and the school experiences of African American students.

Chapter 11 provides a model for analyzing the "discipline event" and building relationships with African American students.

Chapter 12 addresses "reflective leadership," the role of administrators in initiating the change process, and specific strategies are given for changing the school culture or climate.

Chapter 13 focuses on working with parents and the community.

Chapter 14 provides assessments for evaluating the change process and school climate, so that a safe and equitable school is created for all students.

This edition is different in that the focus is equally on both reading and reflecting. The appendices, found in part V, provide a series of reflective exercises after the introduction and each chapter. It is recommended that to gain the most from this book that all exercises are done in sequence and that responders be honest, open, and free to answer with the intention of gaining dynamic understanding of one's beliefs and how these beliefs can influence the way in which the actions and behavior of African American students are perceived.

Racial disparity in discipline has been researched, reported, and discussed since the early days of desegregation; however, the will has not yet been executed on a national scale to change these dynamics. Just consider that at least three generations of African American students in particular have been denied equal educational opportunity despite the promise of the *Brown* decision and the Fourteenth Amendment. Now is the time to act.

Before proceeding to chapter 1, please complete the exercises in Appendices A, B, C, and D.

*Part I*

# The Problem

# ONE

# Racial Disparity in Discipline: A Persistent and Worsening Problem

The mechanisms employed to deny equal educational opportunity to African American students have taken many forms, from de facto segregation to tracking, disproportionate placement in special needs classes, to inadequate funding of schools serving predominately students of color.

Racial disparity in discipline and even the criminalization of African American students began as early as desegregation. In one school, African American males were all seated in what the teacher called "death row." Disproportional, extreme, and unwarranted discipline continues as a major means by which African American students are deprived of educational equity. Whether deliberate or unintentional, African American students are trapped in a vicious cycle that leads to academic failure, dropping out, and being a victim of the school-to-prison pipeline.

Racial disparity in discipline first received national attention when the Children's Defense Fund (1975) reported that black students were two to three times more likely to be suspended than whites; received lengthier suspensions; were more likely to be repeatedly suspended; and were suspended at younger ages.

At the time, it appeared that this phenomenon was merely a symptom of the "growing pains" associated with desegregation efforts. The "burden of fitting in" in desegregated schools was placed largely on black students. Eyler, Cook, and Ward (1983) reported that newly desegregated districts suspended and expelled disproportionate numbers of black students, and black students were more likely to be suspended for "subjec-

3

tive" or "discretionary" offenses (i.e., disobedient, disruptive, or disre-spectful behaviors).

## A PERSISTENT PROBLEM

Almost thirty years after US schools were generally considered to be fully desegregated, racial disparity in discipline continued to be a significant problem. The magnitude of the problem was evidenced by two national studies.

Researchers from the Advancement Project and the Civil Rights Project at Harvard (2000) found that black and Latino students were more likely to be referred for disciplinary actions; to be disciplined for minor conduct; to receive punishments disproportionate to their conduct; and to be referred for discretionary offenses.

The researchers also revealed what would become a disturbing and persistent trend for years to come:

- Out-of-school suspensions for black students was disproportionate to their representation in the school enrollment nationally; black students represented 17 percent of national enrollment but 32 percent of out-of-school suspensions.
- Black males were disciplined more often and more severely than any other minority group.

Skiba, Michael, Nardo, and Peterson (2000) concluded that disproportionate representation of black students in office referrals, suspensions, and expulsions were evidence of pervasive and systematic bias. Their research indicated no evidence that black students acted out more than other students or that racial disparities in school disciplinary outcomes disappeared when controlling for poverty status.

US Department of Education data for the 2004–2005 school year, analyzed by H. Witt in the *Chicago Tribune* (2007), revealed racial inequality in suspensions and expulsions nationwide. The report indicated that:

- In every state except Idaho, black students were being suspended in numbers greater than would be expected from their proportion of the school population.
- In twenty-one states, the disproportionality was so pronounced that the percentage of black suspensions was more than double their percentage of the student body.

- On average, across the nation, black students were suspended and expelled at nearly three times the rate of white students. No other ethnic group was disciplined at such a high rate.

As was found in previous studies, this research indicated that:

- Black students were no more likely to misbehave than other students from the same social and economic environments.
- Poverty alone could not explain the disparities.
- When measured in terms of disciplinary sanctions, such as suspensions and expulsions, schools in the United States remained unequal.

The most disturbing aspect of the report was that only about 6 percent of school districts across the nation acknowledged the issue of racial disparity in discipline and made efforts to address the problem.

Wallace, Goodkind, Wallace, and Bachman (2008) studied large national samples of white, black, Hispanic, Asian American, and American Indian students to examine patterns and trends in racial, ethnic, and gender differences in school discipline. It was found that black, Hispanic, and American Indian youth were slightly more likely to be sent to the office and substantially (two to five times) more likely to be suspended or expelled. Most significantly, they found that although school discipline rates decreased over time for most ethnic groups, school discipline rates among black students increased between 1991 and 2005.

Disturbingly, the most recent federal data indicate that racial disparities in school discipline are growing and that disparities have actually widened. The urgency of the situation is created as African American students are now not only disproportionately being suspended and expelled from school, but arrested or referred to law enforcement as well. The school-to-prison pipeline is alive and well in the US educational system.

Data collected for the 2013–2014 school year by the US Department of Education found that nationally, African American students and students with disabilities were suspended, expelled, arrested, and referred to police at rates disproportionately higher than white or students without disabilities. Analysis of the data showed that:

- African American students were 3.49 times more likely to be arrested at school than white students and more than twice as likely to be referred to law enforcement.
- Students with disabilities were nearly three times more likely to be arrested at school and referred to law enforcement than students without disabilities.

It is crucial to examine disparity among disabled students as the Individuals with Disabilities Act (IDEA) of 1997 found that although African Americans represented only 16 percent of elementary and secondary school students in the United States, they were more likely to be identified by their teachers as having mental retardation than their white classmates by 21 percent.

The most recent data collected for the 2015–2016 school year paints as disturbing a picture. The Civil Rights Data Collection containing detailed information on more than ninety-six thousand public schools found evidence that:

- African American, Hispanic male, and American Indian students face harsher discipline than their white counterparts.
- The number of students being referred to law enforcement authorities and arrested on school grounds or at school activities increased by five thousand from the year before.
- African American students accounted for 15 percent of the student body in the 2015–2016 school year but 31 percent of the arrests.
- Students with disabilities accounted for 12 percent of the enrollment but 28 percent of all arrests and referrals to law enforcement.

Research for more than forty years has indicated that there is no discernable difference in the way African American students behave compared to other students, but racial disparity in discipline has remained consistent (i.e., referrals for subjective offenses, such as disrespect). So, we must ask why. Why is there this persistent separation of African American students from the school setting? But more importantly, why are African American students now being criminalized and forced into the school-to-prison pipeline? As this book goes to press, there is no sign that the problem of racial disparity in discipline is abating.

## THE PRICE OF DISPARITY IN DISCIPLINE

Almost sixty-five years after the *Brown* decision, at least three generations of children have cried out for relief from racism in our schools, but we as educators have failed to hear them. Instead of looking at ourselves and the school environment, we have concluded that single-parent homes, the lack of male role models, television, and rap music are the sole reasons for the enormous discipline gap in our schools today.

Now however, the situation for African American students has become more desperate. Although racial disparity in suspensions has been problematic since school desegregation, the criminalization of African American student is a much more serious issue.

Subjective offenses are a persistent problem, but when talking back to a teacher or disrupting a class becomes a criminal offense (e.g., disorderly conduct) for which a student can be arrested, the consequences for the African American student can be life changing. Arrests lead to detention and confinement in juvenile justice facilities that put the student in direct contact with the criminal justice system.

Racial disparity in discipline is a symptom of a deeper problem that schools must face. It is not an easy issue to address and requires a deeper commitment than designing programs to change student behavior. As educators, we must finally look at how racism manifests itself in the educational system; no more turning a blind eye, making excuses, and not facing our personal, institutional, or national demons related to race.

There is more than forty years of research available related to the problem, but there are no specific strategies provided to solve it. Racial disparity in discipline begins in the mind of the referring party; that mind must be free of the culturally conditioned beliefs that have existed and continue to threaten the education and future of African American students.

This book is intended to address the root causes of racial disparity in discipline through the "Reflective Discipline" approach—a process of gaining awareness, knowledge, and skills that enable teachers, staff, and administrators to view student behavior free of culturally conditioned beliefs and to provide school districts and educators with a "road map" for those who have the will and choose to make a commitment to change.

Go to part V and complete reflective exercises 1.1–1.2.

# TWO

# Persistent Factors Escalating Racial Disparity in Discipline

Zero-tolerance policies and high-stakes testing served as catalysts to fuel racial disparity in discipline. Policies and programs ostensibly meant to curb school violence and increase student achievement worsened school climates for African American students. The lens through which African American students were perceived became more and more clouded. Culturally conditioned beliefs based on stereotypes created statistically proven uneven discipline in classrooms.

Zero-tolerance policies began with the Gun-Free Schools Act of 1994 and was originally created to be a deterrent to bringing weapons to school. To not lose federal funding, the act required states to expel any student who brought a firearm to school for one year. The use of the policy increased dramatically after the Columbine High School shooting in 1999. In addition, school districts used the policy to prevent drug use and violence in school settings.

These policies, which require a specific, consistent, and harsh punishment when rules are broken, began to be applied regardless of the circumstances, the reason for the behavior (i.e., self-defense), and a student's disciplinary history.

Unfortunately, zero-tolerance policies began to be used in schools in ways that mimic the treatment of African American men in the larger society. The same stereotypical images attached to African American men were attached to black boys in the school setting.

Just as black men are watched more closely, arrested for minor offenses such as loitering and disorderly conduct, and given excessively harsh sentences, black boys in particular were referred and disciplined more severely for less serious and more subjective offenses.

Suspension and expulsion rates doubled for African American students in particular as zero-tolerance policies were applied to such offenses as insubordination, swearing, cutting in the lunch line, horseplay, talking back, defiance, and fighting. Zero-tolerance policies soon began to play a major role in perpetuating the school-to-prison pipeline.

Zero tolerance, which was supposed to be "blind justice," became just the opposite for African American students. What was not considered in the application of the policy were the preconceptions and assumptions based on deeply rooted stereotypical images that were the catalyst for the perception of misbehavior and the referral.

## NCLB, RACE TO THE TOP, AND HIGH-STAKES TESTING

Federal educational reforms such as No Child Left Behind (NCLB) and Race to the Top, which focus on high-stakes standardized testing policies, increase the possibility of racial disparity in discipline. Although ostensibly designed to increase the achievement of minorities and to close the racial achievement gap, the policies and practices engendered by high-stakes testing were in fact breeding more failure among the most vulnerable groups. High-stakes testing has only exacerbated the already serious problem of racial disparity in discipline.

The stress imposed by high-stakes testing has increased teacher intolerance for the behaviors of students whose image is already tarnished by racial stereotyping and whose culture is misunderstood or undervalued. Students perceived to be troublesome take away from mandated instructional time and lower test scores. One teacher described the attitudes of his colleagues following a meeting to decrease the number of students being referred as the semester was drawing to a close, "as wanting to be rid of their nuisances for the rest of the year."

The requirements for academic achievement, yearly progress, teacher evaluations, and school "grades" have also heightened the pressure for administrators to remove "troublesome" students. The exit of these students creates the appearance of rising test scores, thus increasing the school's ratings. Zero tolerance provides the means to exclude students perceived to be interfering with the objective of maximizing test scores.

High-stakes testing has also created a climate for students of color who subsequently become the recipients of increased exclusionary discipline.

## TYPE AND PACE OF INSTRUCTION

"Drill and kill joy" instruction, which focuses on "everything that might be on the test," leads to student boredom, frustration, and misbehavior. Students complain about the ubiquitous worksheet and "every day, the same old thing." Often the only excitement that students experience in class is when a student misbehaves.

The pace at which content must be covered is also problematic because when instructional time is allocated by the clock, there is little time to provide help "in the moment." Although students can often receive afterschool tutoring, questions go unanswered, material is not fully understood, and "time-sensitive" explanations of content are lacking.

With high-stakes testing, culturally responsive instruction has been abandoned as "teaching to the test" has become the norm. There is a general disregard for cultural learning styles or instructional approaches that would best suit students from diverse cultures. All of this makes for students whose instructional needs are not met; who become bored, alienated, disengaged from the learning process; and who in turn misbehave in class.

High-stakes testing has produced classroom environments that are rigid and controlled. There is no place for humor or fun. Many young students are now denied time to release excess energy as recess periods have been lessened or totally eliminated in some elementary schools. This sets up boys for disciplinary problems, especially African American boys who tend to be very energetic.

Teachers who are fearful of students, especially African American males, and of losing control of the classroom teach in highly structured and monotonous ways. The type of cooperative learning and group problem solving that most motivates African American students is taboo. Students complain that "they are afraid to let us work in groups because they think they will lose control." Again, with no outlet for creative or well-known adolescent energy, disciplinary events are bound to occur.

## THE ACADEMIC/DISCIPLINE CYCLE OF FAILURE

The "academic/discipline cycle of failure" is played out daily in class-rooms. Most often, the discipline event involves a low-achieving student (for various reasons) and one who may have previously been suspended. The process that occurs as the discipline event is precipitated, developed, and progressed is described.

*Precipitating Event*

- An activity is initiated or introduced that will require student per-formance. The student becomes overwhelmed by a fear of public exposure or ridicule and desires to escape the situation. For in-stance, being called on to go to the blackboard in math class can initiate an event.

*Initiation of Disciplinary Event*

- The student employs a typical ruse or escape tactic (e.g., beginning a conversation with another student, starting to clown around, get-ting up and walking around, claiming to have no pencil or paper, or simply refusing to work).

*Progression of the Disciplinary Event*

- The teacher moves immediately to quell the disturbance. His or her desire is to prevent a disruption that will result in the loss of in-structional time or perceived loss of control. He or she may not understand the student's motivation or be aware of the pattern.
- The teacher writes a referral for the student to be removed from class.

*Consequences of the Disciplinary Event*

- The student is sent to in-school-suspension (ISS) for the class peri-od. He or she escapes the uncomfortable situation and experiences a sense of temporary relief.
- The student fails to get the benefit of instruction for that period or any class work; the teacher may or may not send work to ISS for the student depending on his or her attitude toward the student.

- The student returns to class the next day unprepared, further behind, more frustrated and fearful.
- The cycle repeats.

There is the possibility that the next discipline event involving this student will escalate when the student returns to class. Even though the student was able to escape the discomfort from the previous situation, the student is now further behind and he or she knows it. Additionally, the student is even more fearful and determined to avoid discomfort and embarrassment. This progression of the disciplinary event often occurs in this way:

- Student raises hand to say that he (or she) does not understand. He (or she) is either ignored or told that it is his (or her) fault that he (or she) missed the material.
- The student feels embarrassed now as well as frustrated. He (or she) ups the ante by making some remark to classmates or the teacher.
- The teacher responds with sarcasm or some belittling remark.
- The student feels embarrassed, angry, and perceives that the teacher does not care. The student may use profanity or become disrespectful at this point.
- The teacher writes a referral.
- This time, the student will more likely receive an out-of-school suspension (OSS) for disrespect of the teacher and disruption of the class.
- The student escapes both a humiliating and frustrating situation but falls much farther behind.
- With each discipline event and subsequent suspension, the student's chances of catching up and performing adequately in class are diminished. This pattern will likely continue unless some intervention occurs.

The academic/discipline cycle of failure is the natural result of students missing instructional time; however, with the pressures of high-stakes testing, this cycle has increased. What we do know is that with each suspension, the student falls farther and farther behind, grows more frustrated and angrier, and will more than likely drop out of school.

Educational reforms were designed to increase the academic achievement of students of color and low-income groups, but it is these students who are most vulnerable to all negative outcomes associated with it, especially when it comes to exclusionary discipline. Exclusionary discipline in effect works against all of the good intentions for which educational reforms in the form of high-stakes testing were designed. Instead of creating learning environments in which the academic achievement of many students of color and low-income groups is promoted, it produces another barrier to educational equity.

Perhaps one of the most adverse effects of NCLB, in particular, has been the neglect of the issue of racial disparity in discipline. The Office of Civil Rights' Annual Report to Congress "has aligned its resources to ensure accomplishment of the goals and objectives in the No Child Left Behind Act." Eliminating racial disparities in school discipline was not listed as a priority in OCR's 2002–2007 Strategic Plan (Office of Civil Rights, 2001–2002). The Office of Civil Rights' investigation of allegations of discriminatory discipline policies came to a virtual halt until 2014.

Go to part V and complete reflective exercise 2.1.

# THREE

# New Threats: Adultification and Policing in Schools

The most recent threats to the education, safety, and life chances of African American students are the adultification of African American students and the ubiquitous presence of police, especially in schools primarily populated by poor students and students of color.

Adultification, the newest recognized form of racial profiling and based on culturally conditioned beliefs, is the perception of black children as being more responsible for their actions than children of other groups. The misbehavior of black children is seen as intentional and malicious rather than the mischief or immature decision making of youth.

Adultification denies the childhood innocence of black children as young as kindergarteners; it is a pure form of "dehumanization." Most significantly, a narrative is created at an early age for black children and youth that they are somehow unable to grow and learn from their mistakes.

Zero-tolerance policies and practices allow and encourage the most egregious forms of racial profiling of black children. As a discipline system that mimics the adult criminal justice system, zero tolerance denies black children the protection of childhood. They are punished harshly and excessively for minor and subjective offenses, are given less benefit of the doubt, and are not allowed to be heard. The most recent research affirms the dehumanization in our schools.

Goff, Jackson, Di Leone, Culotta, and DiTomasso (2014) provide evidence indicating that:

- Black boys as young as ten years of age were significantly less likely to be viewed as children than their white schoolmates.
- Black boys are more likely to be mistaken as older, be perceived as guilty, and face police violence if accused of a crime.
- Black boys are seen as responsible for their actions at an age when white boys still benefit from the assumption that children are essentially innocent.

African American men are stereotyped as threatening in this society and are targeted by police even when unarmed. Because stereotypes of black men extend to black boys, their innocence and protection as children is lost. Ultimately, black boys are treated in schools the same way that adult black men are treated in society.

From classrooms to the streets, black boys have never had the childhood right to "just be boys," like white boys. When white boys tussle, it is boys' play; when they cross the line, their actions are viewed as "boyish pranks." When black boys commit the same acts, they are disciplined severely. White boys are able to benefit from the assumption that they are children and essentially innocent and that they will grow up and learn better. Black boys are held for their actions in the same light as a fully grown black male. White boys get time-out counseling; black boys get suspension and jail.

## AFRICAN AMERICAN GIRLS

Although the focus of most research has been related to black boys, new evidence indicates that black girls are as likely to be the victim of dehumanization as males. Two recent studies shed light on the treatment of black girls in our classrooms.

Epstein, Blake, and Gonzalez (2015) and Morris (2016) found patterns in which black girls were viewed as:

- Less innocent and less-childlike than white girls the same age;
- Behaving and seeming older than their stated age;
- Less in need of protection than their white peers;
- More adultlike than white girls;
- Needing less protection and nurturing than white girls;
- Knowing more about adult topics and more knowledgeable about sex than their white peers;

- More independent and more responsible for their offenses;
- Less innocent than their white peers as young as five years of age.
- Implicit racial and gender bias exists when it comes to black femininity;
- There is little room for error when the student is black and female; and
- There is a connection between the stripping of black girls' innocence and the harsher treatment they receive from public school officials and law enforcement.

The results of these studies are deeply disturbing in light of what was found to be the impact of culturally conditioned beliefs and images of black girls. Just as racial stereotypes are held of adult black men and attached to black boys, racial stereotypes of adult black women are attached to black girls.

Stereotypes attached to black women such as being loud, defiant, and oversexualized are similarly associated with black girls. As a result, black girls are more likely to be disciplined for minor infractions like dress-code violations, being disobedient, or disruptive. They are five times more likely to be suspended as white girls and twice as likely to be suspended as white boys.

Most disturbing about the disparity in discipline is the forcing of black girls into the criminal justice system. Although black girls make up slightly less than 16 percent of the female school population, they account for 28 percent of referrals to law enforcement and 37 percent of arrests. Black girls are three times as likely to be referred to the juvenile justice system as white girls. Black girls are 20 percent more likely to be charged with a crime and be detained than white girls. Finally, black girls are less likely to benefit from prosecutorial discretion. The story of Twyla (name changed), which follows, will illustrate the incredible harm being done to young black girls in our schools.

The investigators of the studies reviewed for this chapter have all expressed the recommendation that stereotyping and implicit bias be examined as possible causes of adultification of African American students. Reflective Discipline is a model for initiating that process. Reflective exercises 3.1–3.3 allow the referrer to examine both culturally conditioned beliefs and feelings.

*Twyla's Story*

Twyla, seventeen years old, has been diagnosed with attention deficit hyperactivity disorder (ADHD) and posttraumatic stress disorder (PTSD); she is currently taking medications. She lives with her single mother and two younger sisters in public housing.

> I was having a good day until we went to get on the bus. I got on the bus, went to my seat, number 5, and I sat down. A boy and girl bumped me, and nobody said sorry or excuse me and then I said. Watch where you yall are going. Then the boy started to call me racist names the whole time being on the bus and the bus driver didn't say anything to the boy when he was standing up while the bus was moving. The boy and girl started whispering "I don't know who she is talking to," that's when I ask the girl was it a problem, she didn't say nothing until she got off the bus. Then the bus driver stopped the bus and said I need to do something and then all I remember was her trying to put my seat belt on and then I removed her hand and told her to get out of my personal space. Next thing, I know, her calling the police saying I hit her and her aide on the bus. I sat on the bus for 29 minutes and 36 seconds. When the police came and threw me in a seat and locked me up and took me to the jail. When I went back to school the principal and my teachers was asking was I okay and what happened, but she still driving the bus. She basically lied and I got charged for something I didn't do.

Mother's comments:

> Twyla was charged with battery on a public education employee and placed on probation for six months. During that time, she completed seventy-five hours of community service. She was also placed on house arrest. Both officers from the City police and the Sheriff's Dept. came to her house each night, sometimes twice at night, at all hours to be sure she was in by 8:00 PM. Twyla is now assigned to a program for felony offenders, which meets for three hours a day. It is doubtful that she will be able to graduate on time.

## POLICING IN SCHOOLS

The tragic Marjory Stoneman Douglas shooting in Parkland, Florida, had Americans demanding a solution to school shootings. One strategy favored by state and the federal governments was an increase of policemen in schools. African American students attending Marjory Stoneman

Douglas were not excited about the prospect. They feared that with the elevated security measures, they would be profiled as criminals rather than protected. They suggested that school resource officers (SROs) would need diversity and implicit bias training.

African American students have every right to fear more policing in schools. More SROs pose another serious threat to the educational access and opportunity for African American students. More SROs in schools mean that more black students will enter the criminal legal system in the school as African American students now are already disproportionately arrested in school. African American students, in particular, are arrested for low-level offenses and misdemeanors.

Students of color are more likely to bear the negative consequences of more policing in schools. Although African American students make up only 16 percent of enrollment in our nation's schools, they are 27 percent of students referred to law enforcement and 31 percent of students involved in school-related arrests.

African American students, their families, and communities have legitimate fears of law enforcement. Blacks have a long and bitter relationship with police. According to Hadden (2003) and Kappeler (2014), there are historical reasons for the pattern of racially targeted law enforcement that persists today. Culturally conditioned beliefs of African Americans being criminal and larcenous, along with fears of insurrection assured whites during the enslavement, Emancipation, Reconstruction, and beyond that blacks had to be controlled.

Kappeler (2014) suggests that the institution of slavery and the control of African Americans shaped early policing in America. To regulate the behavior of the enslaved, public slave control systems were established. It was the duty of slave patrols to monitor the movement and behavior of the enslaved, hunt for runaways, look for weapons, and break up meetings of the enslaved.

The slave patrol was the forerunner of modern law enforcement. The language used to describe slave patrols (i.e., "beat" and "patrol") as well as prejudicial attitudes permeated police work long after slave patrols ended. The work of racial control shifted from slave patrollers to modern law enforcement. In some areas of the South, older African Americans refer to whites as "pattys" as in "patty rollers" or patrols.

The oral and collective memories of African Americans for generations is that of negative experiences. Southern policemen, in particular, have been implicated in having relationships with the Ku Klux Klan and in the murders of Civil Rights Workers. The recent killings of African American males by policemen have revived those historic memories. SROs are a constant reminder to African Americans and their children of this bitter history.

Adultification of African American males is of particular concern. In a study of 176 police officers, Goff et al. (2014) reported that police officers overestimated the age of black children, and the culpability of black children was linked to dehumanizing stereotypes. It is critical that SROs on school campuses be trained in the Reflective Discipline process, so that they come to dynamic understanding of the culturally conditioned beliefs that they hold. It is also important that SROs be knowledgeable of the history of law enforcement in the United States, its relationship to the enslavement period, and the reasonable distrust of law enforcement by African American students, their families, and communities.

It is of critical importance that it be remembered that the SRO is usually called to handle a discipline problem at the request of a teacher or administrator. The SRO may not be called to handle a discipline complaint, depending on the perception of and assumption about the student by the referring party.

Images of black adults created in enslavement, Reconstruction, and Jim Crow eras are attached to black children and youth today. These images form the foundation for culturally conditioned beliefs that are perpetuated in our schools. The creation, purpose, and perpetuation of these images will be discussed in chapter 5.

Go to part V and complete reflective exercises 3.1–3.2.

# FOUR

## Reflective Discipline

A teacher's or staff member's perception of student misbehavior and the seriousness of that misbehavior is shaped by deeper mental models. Culturally conditioned beliefs, perceptions of adolescent behavior, and attitudes related to cultural values create the lens through which judgments about student misbehavior are made.

Reducing racial disparity in discipline without addressing the underlying factors as stated previously is an exercise in futility. Programs aimed at improving student behavior have value but cannot and will not address the core issues from which racial disparity in discipline emanate. Unless teachers probe their own beliefs, ingrained patterns of thought and ingrained habits reassert themselves, resulting in the continuing racialization of minor offenses.

Sustainable change in reducing and eliminating racial profiling in school discipline must be transformative. At the deepest levels, teacher and staff belief systems and assumptions—what they believe and feel—must change to create a new lens through which to view the behavior and perceived misbehavior of students of color, especially African American students. It is the referring agent, the teacher, who begins the discipline referral process.

Reflective Discipline is a process of viewing student behavior, free of culturally conditioned beliefs, informed by adolescent development, the developmental issues related to African American students, a sensitivity to cultural norms, and an educational response to student misbehavior.

The Reflective Discipline process involves:

Awareness of:

- The source of culturally conditioned beliefs, how they were reinforced over generations, and continue to be perpetuated.
- How culturally conditioned beliefs about race influence perceptions, assumptions, and attitudes.
- How culturally conditioned beliefs impact feelings about the severity of student misbehavior.

Knowledge of:

- Normal adolescent development and behavior.
- The unique developmental tasks faced by African American adolescents and the factors that influence their identity development.
- African American communication patterns, taboos, and acts that may result in cross-cultural conflict.

Skills in:

- Monitoring and recognizing perceptions and assumptions about African American student behavior and misbehavior that have their roots in culturally conditioned beliefs.
- Identifying and assessing those beliefs and assumptions that guide decisions to refer a student for a disciplinary offense.
- Recognizing feelings attached to those beliefs and thoughts.
- Comparing beliefs and assumptions with research-based knowledge related to adolescent development and, in particular, the developmental issues faced by African American youth.
- Rethinking beliefs and assumptions that run counter to tested knowledge and replacing them with beliefs that will encourage better discipline-related choices.
- Developing empathy for the current life situations of African American students, especially males.
- Increasing sensitivity and responsiveness to cultural differences.
- Appropriate cross-cultural communication.
- Working with African American students to find the best educationally sound solution to correct misbehavior.
- Establishing mutually respectful relationships with African American students that assist in their addressing adolescent identity issues.

Reflective Discipline involves a process of individual self-awareness, self-knowledge, and self-mastery with the intention of becoming a more perceptive, sensitive, and effective educator of all students. The Reflective Discipline process involves the entire school community and is an ongoing process led by a dedicated commitment to the Reflective Discipline process.

Included for each chapter are questions to guide the reflective process. The questions are a practical tool for both individual and group reflection. The Reflective Discipline process challenges all school personnel, including SROs, to create an equitable and safe school culture and climate for all students.

Self-awareness indices are located in the appendices in the back of the book. It is recommended that the reader complete the appropriate self-awareness exercise before reading each of the following chapters.

*Part II*

# The Source of the Problem

# FIVE

# Culturally Conditioned Beliefs

Why has the racial disproportionality of African American students in disciplinary referrals and suspensions continued for almost fifty years? The answer lies in the fact that institutional racism is endemic in our educational institutions and has most often been practiced through the use of the disciplinary process. Culturally conditioned beliefs informed by stereotypical images of African Americans, especially males, have influenced discipline decisions.

For almost four hundred years, stereotypical images of African Americans have flourished in US society. Because of their tenacity and emotional appeal, stereotypes of African Americans have endured and have been reinforced in major societal institutions. Unfortunately, but understandably, our schools, as microcosms of society, harbor the same stereotypes of African Americans.

The beliefs about and attitudes toward African Americans that are prevalent in the larger society exist in the school setting as well. Because stereotypical images of African Americans are part of the cultural psyche of the United States and operate at a programmed unconscious level, administrators and teachers (yes, even good teachers) may respond at an unconscious level to a stereotype. Becoming a teacher does not undo the years of cultural conditioning that all of us undergo.

It is, therefore, not enough to introduce discipline programs that change the behavior of students, while not changing the images that educators hold of a particular group of students. The image that is the impetus for the referral must be examined. Educators must at a very elementary level understand the root cause of the referral (i.e., the image that comes to mind and the belief that stirs the feeling that caused the student's action to be unacceptable).

It is important that educators understand what images fuel their perceptions, how these images came to be part of their conscious and especially their unconscious minds, and how these images influence their behavior toward students.

## STEREOTYPICAL IMAGES OF AFRICAN AMERICANS

Stereotypical images of African Americans have existed since the enslavement of African peoples in this country; they have become as American as apple pie. These images have played a major role in defining US culture and are a significant part of the US cultural belief system.

Rome (1998) states that the previous belief of African slaves as inferior to whites is important to understanding stereotypes because it shapes the ways in which African Americans are perceived today. He states further that it is important to understand the unique experience of African Americans in US history. No other group entered as slaves, and just as important, no other group has been victimized "across centuries" like African Americans because of the original enslaved status.

Why were stereotypical images created? Racial stereotypes did not just appear. They were purposely designed to rationalize the enslavement of Africans and to influence positive beliefs about the enslavement system. The one central message in creating and reinforcing these stereotypes was the inferiority of the African.

Three categories of inferiority were created: intellectual, cultural, and moral. Each and all of the stereotypical images established the rationale for the discriminatory and brutal treatment of African Americans.

The image of intellectual inferiority rationalized enslavement and the menial and subservient place that African Americans would have in the society. Segregated schools, tracking, and the disproportionate placement of African American students in special education, and discrimination in jobs have their roots in the image of intellectual inferiority.

The image of cultural inferiority is reinforced in textbooks that begin the history of African American in slavery, the theory of "cultural deprivation," and the disrespect and disregard for cultural differences.

The image of moral inferiority and the construction of the African American criminal is the most powerful, persistent, and pervasive of all of the stereotypes. The brute stereotype promoted during Emancipation and Reconstruction has gained prominence and today threatens even the education and lives of African American male youth.

**Table 5.1.   Major Categories of African Inferiority and Stereotypical Images**

| Intellectual | Cultural | Moral |
|---|---|---|
| dumb | primitive | untrustworthy |
| childlike | savage nature | loose morals |
| happy | unevolved | predator |
| irresponsible | apelike | menacing |
| mentally inferior | culturally deficient | violent |
| | | dangerous |
| | | aggressive |

## THE CREATION AND PERPETUATION OF STEREOTYPICAL IMAGES OF AFRICAN AMERICANS

These stereotypical images were perpetuated through five major sources in US society: religion, history, social science, popular culture, and the media.

The Bible was used to justify the enslavement of Africans. The story of the curse placed on Canaan by his father, Ham, was most frequently used to justify the moral inferiority and the servile position that the Negro was destined to hold.

History, omitted and distorted, was used to rationalize the enslavement of an "inferior race of people" who had never contributed anything to civilization. Scholars of the period wrote this fake history that was read and taught to generations.

Science and the field of eugenics preached the genetic inferiority of black people. Theories related to the size of the African brain, the thickness of the African neck, eyes white and bulging, and hands hairy and apelike. In many depictions, black images were more animal or apelike than human.

Popular culture, including everything from literature to postcards and toys, created inferior images of blacks, and these images were shared as part of US culture until the Civil Rights movement of the 1960s.

It was advertising that had the greatest impact on making the Southern image of blacks the national image, one that remains in the collective white American mind. Images or pictures are powerful tools that elicit specific emotional reactions from the viewer.

Race is an emotional stimulant. Images that are emotionally saturated, as that of the Negro during that time, have the power to evoke deep emotions in whites and to influence their beliefs over time. These highly distorted images of blacks were created, reinforced, and perpetuated by the former Confederate states for physical, emotional, and social control of the Negro and to maintain a subjugated labor source. The images reinforced the ideology of white superiority and black physical, intellectual, emotional, and cultural inferiority and the belief that blacks were "natural" servants.

## THE MYTHICAL AFRICAN AMERICAN MALE

The most vicious, pervasive, and enduring stereotypes were attributed to African American males (Bireda 2000). Boskin (1986) describes two predominate images of African American men that were developed and flourished almost simultaneously for almost four hundred years: Sambo and the Brute. Both images were derived from the view of African Americans as inferior (for religious, biological, anthropological, or historical reasons) and white Americans both originated these images and used them as a means of maintaining their superior position in society.

Sambo was principally used to present a benign portrait of slavery. Sambo had two principal parts to his nature: he was both childish and comical. Above all, Sambo was amenable to enslavement and to second-class citizenship. This image of the African American male was that of a natural slave-servant. He was nonviolent and humble. He most often played the role of buffoon, displaying outlandish gestures and physical gyrations.

The Sambo image also portrayed the African American male as docile, irresponsible, unmanly, servile, grinning, happy-go-lucky, dependent, slow-witted, humorous, childlike, spiritual singing, and of course, watermelon-eating and chicken-stealing. Sambo was an image of the African American male that provided a measure of psychological safety and security. As long as African American males identified with the image of

Sambo, they were considered to be nonthreatening and were safe from harm to a certain extent.

The Sambo caricature, portrayed as the silly, stupid clown who was afraid of the dark, who was happy despite his condition, who was ever grateful for the paternalism of the enslaver, and who even defended slavery, was created during the early years of slavery and was intensified during the period when slavery was abolished in the North.

With Emancipation and Reconstruction came a new, more threatening image of the African American male. The Brute was born. African American males were portrayed as ignorant, corrupt legislators who stole government money, who pushed whites off sidewalks, and as sexual predators that lusted after white women. In addition, the Brute, because of his violent nature, was thought to be prone to rioting and fighting. The image of the Brute created fear and the need to control the African American male.

The images of the athletic and rhythm-filled African American had their roots in the enslavement period as well. The role that the enslaved were required to fulfill next to that of being a laborer or a servant was that of the entertainer. Enslaved Africans were forced to dance on the slave ships (to exercise the enslaved) and on the auction blocks. On the plantation, dancing, singing, and playing musical instruments were encouraged, rewarded, and often demanded.

Athletics emerged as another aspect of entertainment (Boskin 1986). Enslaved men were often bet upon as they participated in sporting events such as bareback jockeys, boxers, wrestlers, and foot racers. Like the images of the dependent, irresponsible, corrupt, thieving, and violent African American male, the images of the super athlete and entertainer have endured for almost four hundred years as well.

All of these images, as well as other images, were borne out of a particular historical context and were created to justify the status and treatment of African American males. Unfortunately, some variety of these same stereotypes survive today and continue to negatively affect young African American males in all aspects of society, from "driving while black" to disparities in school discipline.

When unconscious stereotyping of African American males occurs in the school setting, it produces biased perceptions and faulty assumptions. These myths and stereotypes generate fear and the need to exercise absolute control of African American males. The resultant tension, misunderstandings, miscommunication, and conflict make it impossible for the African American male students and their teachers to develop rapport or workable relationships. Most often, African American male students become trapped in a cycle of alienation that spirals from disciplinary referrals to suspensions and expulsions to academic failure and dropping out (Bireda 2000).

## THE MYTHICAL AFRICAN AMERICAN FEMALE

Two predominate stereotypical images have existed for African American woman since the enslavement period: Mammy and Jezebel. Over the years, two other negative images, "Sapphire" and the "Welfare Queen" morphed from those images.

Mammy is the fixture of *Gone with the Wind*. She is the ideal enslaved woman. She is obese, dark, grinning, desexualized, and the counter image of Jezebel. Jezebel is an enslaved seductress, a sexual animal, licentious. Jezebel is the overly sexual woman who lures white masters to bed with her, and as a result, mulatto children are born. These two stereotypes created during enslavement have morphed into two equally negative stereotypes of black women.

Sapphire is domineering, strong, tough, and defeminized as well. This overly masculine black image has no feminine traits. She is a modern-day matriarch. The lazy, licentious, scheming Welfare Queen has no ambition other than having babies out of wedlock to secure government assistance to promote her lifestyle.

Just as stereotypical images are attached to black boys, black girls are seen as having an attitude, being loud, and aggressive. They are seen as having no feminine qualities like Sapphire but being overly sexual as Jezebel.

## STEREOTYPICAL IMAGES AND PURPOSE OVER DIFFERENT PERIODS IN AMERICAN LIFE

| Sociopolitical Period | Image | Purpose |
| --- | --- | --- |
| Slavery | Mammy, coon, Sambo, Tom, picaninny | To justify slavery; soothe white consciences |
| Emancipation; Reconstruction | Black peril, Brute, lazy | To justify violence; to eliminate economic competition |

| World War II | Dishonest, immoral | To justify violence; to eliminate economic competition |
| Civil Rights Movement; Black Power Movement, 1950s–1970s | Menace, anti-white, aggressive | To discount and neutralize black activism |
| Modern Racism (subtle vs. open racism); Retreat from the issue of race, 1980s–2018 | Criminal, Drug Dealer, Welfare Queen, Gangbanger | To halt black economic and social progress |

## Modern Racism

Since the Civil Rights movement, into the 1980s and beyond, and the evolution of "modern" racism, the media has been the most potent purveyor of the black male stereotype. The "moral inferiority" of African Americans is the most propagated image in the current American mind. This image of the dangerous black male, the criminal predator Brute produces alarming fear of black males.

Night after night, the image that appears across television screens on the local news is a parade of black men in orange suits. This image of the dangerous black male, which has been transferred to black youth and children who died innocently at the hands of the police, are described as appearing "demon like" (Michael Brown) like twelve-year-old Tamir Rice who appeared to policemen to be older than his youthful years.

## The Nature of Stereotypes

Boskin (1970) states that a stereotype is a standardized mental picture representing an oversimplified opinion or an uncritical judgment that is tenacious in its hold over rational thinking. He further describes stereotypes as:

- being pervasive once implanted in the popular lore.
- an integral part of the pattern of culture that operates within and at most levels of society.
- affecting thoughts and actions at both conscious and unconscious levels.
- operating at reactive levels of thought and action.
- receiving power from repetition.

- very powerful, "often so powerful that they can be dislodged only after a series of assaults on them."

Over time, these stereotypical images become part of the cultural fabric of the society. They become central to the thinking and behavior of the mainstream society toward the targeted group. Most significantly, the erroneous beliefs that result from these images are generally accepted as truth, they are not questioned, and they remain as part of the core belief structure of the larger society, unless changed at an institutional level by the leadership, decree, or mandate. By and large, anyone who grows up in the society is influenced by these beliefs.

## *The Cultural Conditioning Process*

We are born as a tabula rasa or "clean slate." We receive messages from our parents, grandparents, aunts, and uncles, all of the people whom we love and respect, and from whom we learn who we are, the value of our identity, and that of others. When they tell us that a certain group of people is different from us, not as good as us, not to be trusted, or to be avoided, we usually believe them, because these are people that we trust, people who take care of us and meet our needs.

We also receive many significant messages through the social learning context; everything does not have to be stated verbally. Children who are not African American are taught to fear blacks when they are told to check the security of their car doors when they see a group of African American males walking on the street. Anyone who grew up with the Aunt Jemima or Uncle Mose salt-and-pepper shakers learned a lesson, never stated verbally, about the subservient role of African Americans.

By the same token, if the individuals that we are told to respect and honor because they are heroes and leaders give us messages about certain groups through their speeches or writings, those messages also become part of our belief system. When Thomas Jefferson, the quintessential American hero, wrote of the inferiority of blacks, his message became central to the belief system regarding the treatment of blacks in this society.

These beliefs become imprinted at an early age. By age five, beliefs based on myths and stereotypes are already developed, and by age ten, they are imprinted in our consciousness. Unless the cycle is broken, these stereotypical beliefs are passed verbally and nonverbally from one generation to another. Also, unless corrected, generations of students will develop beliefs from textbooks and history lessons based on myths and stereotypes. Through no fault of our own, we inherit a belief system based on stereotypical images.

Eventually, these erroneous beliefs operate at a programmed unconscious level and generate an automatic response. In most instances, when we are reacting to an individual on the basis of a stereotype, we are unaware of it. This unconscious, programmed nature of stereotypes makes them so difficult to change.

Modifying erroneous beliefs will occur only through examining these beliefs at a conscious level, monitoring one's behavior, and practicing positive conscious beliefs. It is not enough to know that stereotypes influence perceptions and assumptions, it is crucial that educators examine the historical roots of racial stereotypes.

These stereotypes are endemic in US society; they have a pervasive quality to which no one is immune, not even the victims of stereotyping themselves. Because of their persistent and pervasive quality, as educators, we must examine any culturally conditioned beliefs that we may unconsciously hold about African Americans in this society.

Go to part V and complete cognitive restructuring exercise 5.1.

# SIX

# The Impact of Culturally Conditioned Beliefs and Images

When unconscious stereotyping in the form of adultification occurs in the school setting, faulty assumptions, false accusations, and fear are commonplace. Miscommunication takes place, tension mounts, and conflicts between teachers and African American students result.

Stereotyping most often produces predictable results in the form of self-fulfilling prophecies and always leads to tension and conflict in the classroom. First, in most instances, at an unconscious level, the teacher or administrator holds a stereotypical image and related erroneous belief about the African American student. Second, an event occurs in the classroom that elicits an automatic response from the teacher. Third, this response elicits an immediate reaction from the student. Fourth, the student's reaction confirms the belief held about the student and reinforces the stereotype.

The comments of one principal are an indication of the type of interactions that occur with African American students. When an African American male was given a referral, the principal remarked with obvious glee, "Ah ha! We've got him now." She had been annoyed for some time by what she considered his defiant attitude. The student was enraged by the principal's comment and proceeded to tell her so. The more the student vented, the more vindicated the principal felt. The student was now proving what she had always believed.

As was stated previously, African American male students, in particular, are the victims of differential treatment that occurs because of stereo-

37

typing. They face similar experiences in school, as do older African American males in the larger society.

If we fear African American males on the streets, we fear them in the hallways; if we follow African American males in stores because we believe they are thieves, then they become the "usual suspect" when something is missing in the classroom. Also, as in the larger society, when the African American male steps outside of his prescribed role, when the African American student asserts his manhood and defends his integrity, he is severely punished.

When teachers are more comfortable with the Sambo image of African American male students, they relate better to the jovial, playful African American male than the serious, quiet one who is perceived to have an "attitude." The Sambo image also creates greater acceptance for the African American male student who is submissive rather than assertive, the latter being perceived as aggressive or defiant (Bireda 2000).

When teachers see the African American male as the Brute, they respond to him with fear; they are afraid to admonish him or to wake him when he sleeps in class. The Brute image leads to a preoccupation with control and unjust labeling. He is punished most often for minor offenses (Bireda 2000).

Described next are the consequences of cultural conflicts and stereotyping in the classroom.

## UNREALISTIC EXPECTATIONS: ADULTIFICATION

We tend to hold African American students to much higher standards of behavior than we do other groups of students. In fact, developmental norms are literally "thrown out of the window" when it comes to African American students, especially males. We never allow African American males, in particular, the luxury of "being boys." They are routinely more harshly punished for misbehavior that is considered normal for youngsters.

These unrealistic expectations begin in kindergarten when young males with high energy levels (like most healthy boys their age) do not sit still and are labeled hyperactive. When young African Americans get off the bus, in many instances after long bus rides, they are expected (in the words of one African American teacher) "to walk like little soldiers" to the building. African American adolescents, like others their age, are ruled more by hormones than clear thinking.

Much of the "misbehavior" for which African American males in particular are punished severely is typical of youth their age. From the first day of school, the control of African American males begins. They are punished more often and more severely for the typical misbehavior of children and youth their ages.

## FAULTY ASSUMPTIONS

On many occasions, teachers are quick to assume that a misdeed is intended on the part of the African American male, when his actions are really quite innocent. The stereotype of the oversexed black male looms just beneath the surface. The following two examples of this involve very young African American males.

In one instance, a young male had been given a pair of 3-D glasses. He had spent the evening pretending to see through plants, walls, clothing, and the like. The next day, he took the glasses to school (which he should not have been allowed to do). He told a white classmate, "I can see through your clothes." The teacher overheard the comment and referred the student to the office for "sexually inappropriate behavior." The parents were livid and explained that there was no sexual intent in his statement; he merely meant that his 3-D glasses could penetrate all types of surfaces, including clothing.

In another case, a young African American boy went to the bathroom, forgot to zip his pants, and came out. One of his white female classmates told the teacher, who then referred the young boy to the office for "sexual harassment." His parents could not understand why the teacher could not have simply told their son to zip his pants.

On occasion, Caucasian female teachers have spoken of African American males "exuding sexuality" or sensing a type of "sexual come-on" on the part of African American males, which produces a type of "sexual tension" between them and the student that they find uncomfortable.

Faulty assumptions especially about the "innate badness" of poor African American children often deny them the opportunity to receive much-needed support services. As the author has interviewed and worked with African American students who were frequently suspended from school, it was discovered that many of them were experiencing severe personal and family problems.

Some were having the typical disagreements with parents, holding deep resentment toward an absent father, or experiencing traumatic life events. One student in particular who was repeatedly in trouble and suspended was in great need of grief counseling as he had gone home from school to discover his deceased mother. Many other students who were repeatedly suspended from school were obviously depressed. When faulty assumptions are made about students, punishment is the first course of action, and their need for counseling or other intervention is neglected.

## BEHAVIOR TRACKING

In the same way that African American students are tracked academically, they are tracked behaviorally. First of all, we expect these students to misbehave, and when they do, they enter a track they cannot escape. They will never start another day "tabula rasa"; he is tarnished. He will get no breaks and no second chances because once he misbehaves, he wears a label.

In some cases, teachers keep a file to document the misbehavior of certain students. For example, one teacher pulled out a file that she keeps on an African American male student in particular; she says that one of the first things she does each day is to date a sheet of paper and wait for him to misbehave because she knows he will.

The result of behavior tracking comes in the words of an African American mother who was distressed because her son had dropped out of school. She begged him not to, but he said that he could not take it anymore because "they won't let me change." Another student commented, "I am trying to change, but it seems like it's no use. Sometime, I don't even want to come back."

## INCONSISTENCY

One of the complaints heard most often from African American males and their parents is that discipline is inconsistent; in their words, "there are different rules for different students." Many of the complaints of racism come from the student's perception that non–African American and middle-class students are not punished or are not punished as severely as are African American males. African American students are aware of any inconsistencies and are always watching to see if a teacher is going to be fair in administering consequences for misbehavior.

African American parents indicate that they want their children punished when they misbehave, but that they want the same rules that apply for their children to apply to all others. In a workshop, a teacher told how he had come to a level of greater awareness with regard to consistency in discipline. He had admonished two African American students for their behavior and said that the next person to make a sound is "out of here." Well, the next person to make a sound was a Caucasian male student who simply said "e." At that moment, the teacher said that he saw and felt the eyes of every African American student in that room because they were all waiting to see if he would be true to his word and send the Caucasian out of the classroom. He said that until that day, he never knew the extent to which African American students observed their teachers to see if they were consistent in applying the rules.

Students who attend predominately African American schools report favoritism based on student grades or attitudes. They feel that some students get away with a lot, while others are "targeted." One young man stated, "I see others doing things, if it were me, I would get the worse consequences."

## LEADING BEHAVIORS

In many cases, African American males are "set up" for misbehavior. The teacher knows which "button to push," so that the student "goes off" or becomes verbally abusive. The set-up technique is often used by some teachers when they do not wish to have a student in their class on a particular day or any day.

In this case, the teacher simply says whatever he or she knows will upset the student to the point that he (or she) reacts and is subsequently sent to the office. Lacking maturity, these students never seem to understand that this is a ploy. African American male students often complain, however, that often they "feel like they are in a constant battle."

Teacher provocation is the one behavior that African American males most report. Here are some of the comments that express their feelings about teacher actions in this regard.

- "I can tell she doesn't want me in the class. She wants me to withdraw. She keeps coming at me; eventually I break down and get kicked out."
- "If you ask a question, she looks at you like you are a fool; it makes you want to say something to her, tell her about herself."
- "Our conflict began on the first day of school when I pulled my shirt out before I left the building. Since then, he has been trying to provoke me. Little slick things; the least little thing to get me out of class."

Finally, this event was in a classroom. These comments were made by the teacher to one student in the span of a few seconds.

- "Fix your clothes." (He tucked his shirt in.)
- "Get your feet off the back of the chair." (He did.)
- Stop calling out the answer." (Student had been raising his hand but was ignored.)
- "Open your eyes." (He replied, "my eyes ain't closed.")
- She corrected his speech.

## PERSONAL DISREGARD

Because African American students are expected to be lazy and irresponsible—to not care about their schoolwork or getting an education—in some ways, they become invisible. They often complain that they are ignored and not listened to. Most often, they complain of being disrespected. Many times, they feel that they are not listened to or respected until they "go off." The African American male, considering his position in society, is sensitive to what he perceives to be disrespect. Some feelings expressed by African American males about what they consider to be disrespect follow.

- Student was wearing a T-shirt of a prohibited color (yellow) underneath his outer uniform shirt. "She tried to embarrass me in front of everyone. Why did she have to yell at me? She could have just asked me to button up."
- "My teacher is just rude." He recounts these two incidents: "When a student didn't have paper, teacher says: "If you can buy designer clothes, you can buy paper."

- When students were allowed to share snacks, teacher says to one student, "We don't want any of that food stamp food."
- "She interrupts me, won't listen to me. She gets thirty minutes [to make her point], and I get two seconds."
- "At least listen to me, let me explain. It didn't happen like that."
- "I snap when I feel disrespected, yelled at, just talk to me."
- "Talk to me with respect; it makes me angry, we are both human. Pull me to the side."

There is the belief that African American students only respond to harsh treatment; that they do not understand anything else. There is a difference between firm and harsh and disrespectful behavior toward a student. If students come from a home background where harshness is the norm, that is even more reason to teach them a better way of interacting with others.

## FAILURE TO TAKE ADVANTAGE OF TEACHABLE MOMENTS

Discipline involves both punishment and teaching. The focus of most disciplinary action with African American males is punishment. African American parents often ask why the school official did not talk to their son and explain to him why what he did was wrong. An African American parent volunteer in the school bookstore observed the way in which two incidents involving the theft of a pencil from the bookstore were handled by a teacher.

In the first instance, an African American male stole a pencil and was immediately referred to the office for ISS. In the next instance, involving the same teacher, a Caucasian male stole a pencil. However, rather than being referred to the office, he was given a lecture on why it was wrong to steal. The volunteer felt that it was assumed that African Americans would steal and the little boy had to be "taught a lesson," whereas the stealing on the part of the Caucasian student was considered to be a less serious matter.

There are other times when teaching is the most effective approach. An African American high-school student referred to one of his favorite teachers as "his dog" and was overheard by an administrator. The administrator became angry and admonished the student to never use that term again. The student was confused and felt embarrassed and put down by the administrator.

A better way to have handled the situation would have been to make this a teachable moment and explain to the student that some terms, although appropriate to use when referring to and communicating with one's peers, are considered inappropriate in the school setting. In this way, the student would have learned a valuable lesson without undermining his self-esteem.

## FAILURE TO ACKNOWLEDGE AND RESPECT CULTURAL DIFFERENCES

Stereotypes get in the way of acknowledging and respecting cultural differences. When one's beliefs about African American males are based on negative stereotypical images, it is more difficult to view differences as differences rather than deficits.

Excessive noise is often an offense for which African American males are referred. In these cases, the African American male will be viewed as loud and emotional because he is considered to be uncouth and untrained. Often his failure to establish direct eye contact will be considered to be a sure indicator of his dishonesty.

## EXCESSIVE PUNISHMENT

A common complaint of African American parents is that the punishment often far exceeds the offense. There appears to be a belief that because of innate character deficits and a proclivity for thievery, fighting, and disruptive behavior, African American males who break the rules should be "made examples of" to warn all others that this behavior will not be tolerated.

In one case, an elementary school student who was "clowning around" in the cafeteria was publicly paddled over the school intercom. In another instance following Halloween, a high-school teacher allowed his class to eat candy in class. An African American male threw the stick from a lollipop out of the window. The student was told to do one hundred push-ups and warned that if he stopped, he would be made to start over. The student said that he would not do one hundred push-ups because he physically could not do one hundred push-ups (he was slight in build). The student was referred for insubordination.

Some punishment serves no real purpose, in that it does not correct behavior; for instance, when students, in some cases, are rewarded for cutting class or being tardy by being suspended. One student who had excessive tardiness, twenty-two to be exact, was suspended for one day; he was suspended another two days for missing his fourth block class; and then ultimately ended up with five days out-of-school suspensions for cutting class on two other occasions.

Repeated behaviors such as tardiness or cutting class are symptomatic of deeper problems, indicating that intervention is needed. Allowing a student to have one- and two-day vacations from school does nothing to address the problem and, more significantly, contributes to the academic/discipline cycle of failure.

Finally, the criminalization of student misbehavior is rampant, especially in predominately African American schools. Students who fight are arrested and those who witness and do not report a fight are often suspended as well.

## INTOLERANCE FOR VIOLATION OF "GROUP-ASSIGNED" BEHAVIORS

The purpose of stereotyping is to control the targeted group, so stereotypes are always accompanied by a code or set of rules by which the victim of the stereotype must abide. These rules regulate the personal behavior of the targeted group.

There has always been a written and unwritten code of behavior for African American males that, like the stereotypes themselves, has been transmitted from generation to generation. Like stereotypes, these codes operate at an unconscious level; without our awareness, they can influence our reactions to certain behaviors in African American males. When African American males violate this historical code, they are usually severely punished.

Five of the major historical or black codes that governed the behavior of African American males and the interpretation of the violations of these codes in the modern-day school setting follow.

1. **Three or more black males shall not gather.** It was originally felt that if blacks were allowed to congregate, they might conspire against the enslavers. The sight of black men gathering created fear in whites. Today, the sight of three or more black males still pro-

duces fear. Often, black males walking down the hall or sitting together in the cafeteria can create feelings of uneasiness.

2. **Never strike a white.** Blacks have always been severely punished for striking whites. Black parents often complain that their son was punished more severely when he was involved in a fight with a white student. In many cases, the black male is punished for starting a fight when he strikes a white student for using the "n" word. Most often, the white student remains unpunished for the use of the word; what happens, in effect, is that the original victim of racial harassment and verbal assault now becomes the perpetrator of the offense.

3. **Never raise your voice at a white.** When the black male becomes emotional, his behavior is considered to be verbally aggressive or disruptive. In many cases, his volume increases when he is attempting to state his case or defend himself.

4. **Never contradict a white.** When black males feel that they are being treated unfairly, they will insist on "being heard." This behavior usually gets them into trouble and the student is labeled argumentative, insubordinate, or defiant.

5. **Be submissive.** When black males are not submissive in speech or manner, they risk the danger of getting into real difficulty. They are assumed to have an "attitude." This lack of submission is usually met with a show of power with the intention of showing them who is in control. Even black males who are excellent students get into trouble when they do not display humility or act "too proud." This "attitude" is what seems to be most offensive to many teachers and administrators.

A middle-class African American teacher recalled how her two sons were treated differently in the school setting. The oldest one, the smarter of the two, is serious, does not joke or play around, and is considered by his teachers to have an attitude. His younger brother, who is not as bright academically, is more outgoing and jovial. He is considered an ideal student and has never had a discipline problem. The mother of these two students is certain that her elder son's lack of submissiveness is what causes problems for him at school.

The belief that the African American male must be controlled is based on the historical image of the Brute. The need to exercise control and to demonstrate authority is one of the major causes of tension, conflict, and disciplinary problems involving the African American male student.

When a "show of power" is used unnecessarily, it will provoke a negative reaction in the African American male student. He will most definitely strike back when he feels that he is challenged, humiliated, ignored, or treated unfairly. This, of course, creates a lose–lose situation in the classroom. The African American male student will most definitely lose because he will face some type of disciplinary action. The teacher also loses, however, because students are always watching, and they will lose respect for the teacher who must exercise power in this manner.

African American students, in epidemic proportions, are being trapped in a cycle that leads to disciplinary referrals, detention, ISS, expulsion, or placement in an alternative setting. This cycle ultimately ends with academic failure and dropping out. For many, the future is even more bleak: incarceration is the last stop in the cycle.

The belief that African American students and males in particular must be controlled gets at the heart of the matter of racial disparity in discipline as relates to these students. The school culture and climate determine what the experience of the African American student will be in either a predominately mainstream or predominately ethnic minority school.

Go to part V and complete reflection exercises 6.1–6.3.

# SEVEN

# African American Cultural Patterns: Cultural Conflicts and Disciplinary Practices

Senseless and inappropriate referrals are given to African American students because of cultural blindness (lack of knowledge of the culture) and cultural insensitivity (lack of respect for the culture). Although both males and females are affected, African American females may be the targets of much of disciplinary actions related to cultural patterns, especially as it relates to dress codes and ethnic hairstyles.

## CULTURAL CONFLICTS IN THE CLASSROOM

Even if the African American student is acknowledged as having a culture, and one that is simply different, not defective, he or she faces yet another challenge. As Greenfield, Raeff, and Quiroz (1996) suggest, the customary modes of activity and interaction (of minority students) often differ from those favored by the mainstream Euro-American culture in public schools.

Although African Americas are not a monolithic ethnic group, with all members being attached to traditional cultural norms to the same degree, it can be safely stated that African American students generally must give up significant aspects of their cultural identity to be successful in the US public-school system. Independence and individual achievement, aspects of the core mainstream value of individualism, with Anglo-Saxon and

European immigrant origins, is highlighted in the cultural–institutional setting of US schools.

Greenfield et al. (1996) suggest that this contrasts with the collectivistic cultural value orientation (which emphasizes interdependence) of many non-Western immigrants and minority groups (i.e., Asian Americans, Hispanics, African Americans, and American Indians). According to Greenfield et al., children from individualistic and collectivistic value orientations become adept at different modes of activity and have different conceptions of appropriate behavior.

The behavioral aspects associated with the collectivistic value orientation of African Americans (e.g., grouping behavior, the "we," social and cooperative orientations when misunderstood) can be precipitating factors for disciplinary actions involving African American students.

The grouping behavior of African American students can be threatening and intimidating to some teachers in the school setting. The communalism value is held and practiced strongly by African American students, especially in situations where they might be in a numerical minority population. It is important to bond, to stick together, and even to protect each other if necessary.

Sitting together in the cafeteria, at sporting events, and even walking together down the hallways is very important to African American students. This grouping, plus the emotional nature of African American communication (perceived to be loud), often calls attention to African American students. The problem occurs when African American students feel that they are unduly being singled out or harassed when they see other groups engaging in the same behavior.

The "we" orientation is also exhibited in conflict situations. When African American males hear about or see what they believe to be mistreatment or harassment of another African American, especially by an outsider, they assume a protective stance, which often leads to fights.

Not only do African American males feel the obligation to protect other African Americans from students from other groups but from teachers as well, if necessary. African American male students often get into trouble by coming to the defense of another student when they feel the teacher is mistreating or picking on that student. In this situation, the responsibility to the group transcends the individual consequences that may result from this action.

The social orientation of African American students tends to make them appear more interested in socializing than in doing schoolwork. African American students are often written up for wasting time, not completing work, and excessive talking.

This social orientation is most important, however, in the teacher–student relationship. African American students have a high need to connect with the teacher and to feel that the teacher accepts, respects, and cares about them as an individual. African American students are intuitively aware of the teacher's genuineness and caring. The quality of the teacher–student relationship will determine the extent to which discipline problems will occur with African American students.

The cooperative spirit of African American students is often misinterpreted as cheating. African American students distinguish between actual cheating and helping a friend find the page or "assisting" another student who is having a problem. Other values related to culturally influenced personality traits can also be precipitating factors for conflict in the classroom.

The value of expressive individuality, which is interpreted as style and demonstrated in the fads in clothing, hairstyles, and mannerisms, can cause major problems especially for African American students. African American males in particular are found to express their individuality in ways that are unacceptable in the school setting.

The wearing of too-large pants, not wearing belts, and the showing of underwear are all unacceptable in the school setting. The wearing of sunglasses and hats indoors, which is inappropriate according to mainstream and school etiquette, is considered totally acceptable by many African American males.

Sometimes, a style of wearing clothing, such as one pant leg up or males wearing cornrows, is incorrectly attributed to gang affiliation. A major cause of conflict between African American students and the administration occurs when students feel they are falsely labeled as gang members.

## THE CULTURALLY BASED ISSUES OF
## AFRICAN AMERICAN FEMALES

The value of expressive individuality, which is interpreted as style and demonstrated in the fads in clothing, hairstyles, and mannerisms, can cause major problems for African American female students. African American girls are most often disciplined for subjective infractions like dress-code violations including ethnic hairstyles and being disruptive.

African American females are especially impacted by culturally destructive norms and policies in schools. African cultural retentions such as ethnic hairstyles (i.e., afros, braids, and locks as well as head coverings) are legitimate aspects of African American female culture. Hair in particular is a form of personal expression, a source of ethnic pride, and even social consciousness. To individuals with West African cultural roots, hair has social, aesthetic, and spiritual significance. Braided designs, unique hairstyles, and hair adorned with cloth, beads, and shells are forms of cultural expression for African American females.

One of the core African American values is that of preferring novelty, freedom, and personal distinctiveness, especially in clothing styles. This value, which helps define one's identity during the crucial stages of adolescent development, is attacked through dress-code policies in schools.

The socialization pattern of African American females is one of independence and speaking their minds. This assertiveness is considered to be aggressive and unladylike by teachers whose own cultural norms require different standards of femininity. The culture of discipline in our schools places African American girls in double jeopardy; they are both black and female.

In the next chapter, we will deal with the aspect of culture that causes the most problems for African American students in the classroom: their communication style. It should be noted that some of the cultural preferences in communication styles will also be relevant to other students from collective cultures (i.e., eye contact, emotional expression, etc.).

Go to part V and complete reflective exercise 7.1.

# EIGHT

## Cross-Cultural Communication Conflicts: African American Communication Patterns

African American culture is an oral culture. Great significance is placed on the oral transmission of information. Traditionally, African beliefs, values, customs, and history were transmitted by word of mouth from generation to generation. In African American culture, great respect is afforded those who possess exceptional verbal skills. If one examines the leaders whom African Americans have chosen to listen to, they are, without exception, great orators.

The significance placed on oral skill in African American culture is so important that a major part of the socialization process, especially for African American males ages eight to fifteen, is the rite of passage associated with learning and using the language of the culture.

Hale-Benson (1986) describes an important manhood rite for African American males, playing the dozens, an activity engaged in primarily by young men in which two opponents duel verbally. Derogatory comments are made about each other, and their respective family members, especially the mother. The successful player masters several competencies, including being able to think quickly and to control his emotions. This culturally approved and respected verbal skill causes special problems for African American males in the school setting.

According to Dandy (1991), African American males speak a particular kind of stylized talk; learning how to use this talk is an essential part of passage from boyhood to manhood; teachers generally are unfamiliar with the rules, purpose, and intent of this stylized talk; and often the students who use this talk are referred by teachers to remedial classes, special-education classes, or classes for behavior disorders. The manner and tone in which some African American male students, in particular, communicate is often considered to be disrespectful and even intimidating by some teachers.

## CULTURALLY BASED COMMUNICATION PREFERENCES

Each of the following communication preferences can create tension and cause conflict if not understood and respected.

### Call and Response

This communication pattern is seen in African American churches when African Americans listen to speakers. It is permissible and expected that one responds verbally to a speaker; this usually indicates approval for what the speaker is saying and encourages the speaker to continue in the same vein. For instance, in church, it is permissible to say "Amen" or "say it" back to the preacher. When African Americans hear the speaker say something that they like, it is permissible to say "tell it like it is" or something similar to encourage the speaker.

The "silence is golden" that appears on the screen and is expected in the movie theater does not have the same impact for some African American moviegoers who customarily "talk back to the characters on the screen." One might hear "You tell him, girl!" or "Don't go in there!" to warn a character in the movie. Verbal disapproval is also allowed in some settings, for instance, at talent shows, where the audience indicates its disapproval through hoots, grunts, and the like.

This African American cultural form is foreign to, and disapproved of, in the school setting. The school rule is to sit quietly and listen to the speaker. Interrupting the speaker with encouraging or disapproving remarks is taboo. African American students who "forget where they are" and respond in this manner are considered to be rude and out of line. The student's response and feeling on the other hand, is "All I said was. . . ." He then feels angry and that the teacher is "picking on him." When African American students feel that they are being ignored when their hands are up, they will often yell out the answer, which can earn them a referral.

## High-Context Communication

African Americans are known as high-context communicators. They are not word-bound, and as such, derive as much meaning from what is not said verbally (the nonverbal cues) as from what is stated. African Americans watch the facial expressions, body movements, the stance, and even the changes in complexion when assessing a situation. African Americans place a high value on being genuine and "real," and use the nonverbal cues as indicators of genuineness.

When an African American student says that a particular teacher does not like him or her or that a teacher is prejudiced, the student is usually basing his beliefs on intuitive feelings and nonverbal cues. This, of course, often makes the African American student appear as though he or she is using the "race card" or "race as an excuse" because members of mainstream culture tend to use information obtained from words and the senses (rather than intuition) to make judgments.

## Emotional Expression

African Americans are "high-keyed" communicators, which means being loud and emotional when talking about something that they are interested in or have strong feelings about. When talking about something that is important to them, students may become excited and animated. When they are engaging in a debate, they may express their opinions in a loud and emotional manner, even though they are not angry. Many times, outsiders to the African American culture may feel that African Americans are venting anger or hostility when they are heard arguing a point.

The loud and emotional manner in which African American males and females communicate is threatening and intimidating to teachers who do not understand this communication style. Teachers will often send students to the office because they fear a fight is going to break out, when in actuality, the students are only engaging in a verbal game of "sellin' wolf tickets" (loud, threats).

When African American males and teachers are involved in a conflict situation, especially when the male feels he has been unjustly accused or has not been able to state his case, he may become louder and more animated. This is not an indication that he is ready to strike the teacher, only that he is trying harder "to be heard."

## AREAS IN WHICH CULTURAL CONFLICTS CAN OCCUR

### Distance

The relationship that one has with an African American determines how close one gets to him or her in a conversation. Individuals from outside the culture are usually not permitted to get as close unless a relationship exists with that person. In a conflict situation, it is appropriate to maintain a distance of at least three feet or arm's length. The comment "don't get in my face" indicates that one is violating an individual's space. (Recall the bus driver and Twyla from chapter 3.)

Often, to show power and authority, a teacher will get into an African American student's face. This is a major cultural taboo for African Americans; it is considered a challenge and will be treated as such. If the teacher does not respond to the student's warning to get out of his face, then the student will probably resort to some physical means to protect his "space."

### Physical Contact

In the midst of a conflict, any movement touching the other individual is considered provocation. Two African American individuals may engage in a loud and emotional argument but may be nowhere near fighting unless one of them makes a provocative move. This move is usually an indication that one must protect oneself.

When teachers touch or push or move students along, the student's response is usually "don't touch me." In some cases, the student will view the touching as provocation and respond in a physical manner. Again, as in the case of distance, a "relationship" will make the difference.

### Eye Contact

Traditionally, African American children have been taught to lower the gaze to show respect and humility for parents and other adults. To stare at an adult is considered rude and is taboo. There are some African American parents, however, who teach their children to hold their heads up and look everyone in the eye as a means of maintaining their dignity.

A problem arises when the teacher attempts to force an African American student to make eye contact when the student was taught to lower the gaze to show respect. Contrary to the belief of some teachers, an African American student's lowering of the eyes does not mean that he or she is lying or trying to hide something. It also is not an indication of low self-esteem in this instance.

Many teachers who need to exert their power through attempting to force eye contact insist that they only do this because African American students must learn to establish eye contact in the job market. It is important to separate the two; forcing a student to make eye contact in a conflict situation is not the same situation as a job interview and can only lead to an escalation of the conflict.

### Gestures

African Americans find the direct pointing of fingers to show authority and finger-snapping to get one to move to be inappropriate. When a teacher puts his or her finger in the face of an African American male in particular or snaps fingers to move him along, it is considered insulting, and the student will usually respond in a negative manner.

## CULTURAL TABOOS

- Asking personal questions, shaming in public, and the use of the terms "boy," "girl," and "you people" are highly offensive to African Americans of any age and are considered derogatory terms. African Americans have a concept of "my business" and are often suspicious when individuals appear to be too interested in their personal lives.
- Young African American males find "boy" to be particularly offensive and will ask a teacher whom she or he is talking to if addressed as "boy."
- Public shaming is a definite taboo; when an African American male is shamed in front of his classmates, he will take the shaming as a challenge as well as an insult and will defend both his manhood

and his dignity. Public shaming on the part of a teacher can only lead to a lose–lose situation. The student will invariably be punished for the outbreak that will occur after the incident, and the teacher will lose the trust and respect of the other students who observed the incident.

If teachers can become aware of and respect the cultural rules relating to communication styles, tension between teachers and African American male students will decrease; conflicts can be avoided and incidents will not escalate.

## CULTURAL ETIQUETTE

The social forms to be observed in interactions with individuals from diverse cultural backgrounds are cultural etiquette. There are rules that govern all of our interactions with others and rules for interacting with those who may come from backgrounds different from our own.

What follows are some rules for interacting with African American students in the classroom, especially in conflict situations. When teachers follow these rules, they show a respect for the culture, the communication preferences, and taboos of African American students. These rules relate to each of the communication elements previously discussed.

- Call and Response: Do explain that there are different types of responses that are appropriate for different kinds of activities. Allow students to establish rules for when a more culturally based style can be used—for example, when discussing current events or some political issue.
- Distance: Do not get in student's face. Maintain an acceptable distance (about an arm's length), especially when in the midst of a conflict.
- Physical Contact: Do not touch student, especially in the middle of a conflict situation. If students need to leave the room, give a friend permission to walk outside the room with and talk to student until he or she cools down (all with the student's permission, of course).
- Eye Contact: Do not force student to establish eye contact. Not looking at you does not necessarily mean that student is lying, trying to hide something, or being defiant.

- Gestures: Do not point your finger in student's face or snap your fingers at him or her.
- Emotional Expression: Do not assume that the student is going to hit you or someone else if he is loud and animated. Most important-ly, give him the opportunity to be heard, to defend himself, and to state his case. Doing this simple thing will decrease conflict with African American males to a significant extent. Also, learn to distin-guish when he is strongly expressing an opinion or arguing the "principle of the thing" from when he is angry.
- High-Context Communication: Listen to him when he says that he feels that you do not like him. Do not become defensive if he says that he feels you are prejudiced. Ask him what makes him feel this way. Do some self-reflection and determine how you feel about him and why.
- Cultural Taboos: Never call him "boy." Most importantly, never shame him in public. Ask him to step aside or right outside the door to speak to him. Ask him if you two can spend some quality time talking about the issue later so that the problem can be re-solved.

## AVOIDING THE ESCALATION OF DISCIPLINE EVENTS

A "perceived insult" is often the precipitating factor when a miscommu-nication escalates into a full-blown discipline event. The student, usually an African American male, perceives that he or a classmate has been insulted or disrespected by the teacher. The violation of some cultural norm is usually what causes the student to react; he feels that he must defend his honor or that of a classmate.

When African American males are asked how a particular situation could have been avoided, they often respond: "If she had just asked me to be quiet, she didn't have to yell at me?" or "Why did he have to get in my face?" Sometimes a student reacts to repeated admonitions to "look at me!"

The cultural violation, the student's perception, and his defense set into motion an event that escalates and ends with the student being sent to OSS or worse, depending on the level to which the event escalates. A typical event that escalates follows.

Teacher (Yells at student): "I told you to sit down!"

Student: "Why you got to yell at me?" (Other students laugh)

Teacher (Disregarding student's response, yells again): "Sit down, mister! I'm not telling you again."

Student: "Why you acting like that? What's wrong with you? Don't you see me going to my seat?"

Teacher: "That's it, buddy; you are out of here." (Approaches student to move him along.)

Student: "Get your hands off me!"

Teacher: "What did you say to me? Who do you think you are talking to?"

Student: "I said 'keep your hands off me.'"

Teacher, angered by student response and starting to feel threatened, calls for officer to come and take student from room.

Student: "I didn't do nothing, you jokey."

Teacher: "I'll add that to your referral. You are out of here."

Student: "F*** you!"

The escalation of this event could have been avoided by the teacher adhering to cultural rules that governed the communication with this student. Yelling at him, ignoring his comments, and approaching him all helped to escalate the event.

The term "you jokey" used by students at a high school means "you can't be serious" and is taken personally by teachers. Students frequently use the term and are just as often sent to ISS for its use.

Perceived insult or disrespect is a sensitive issue for African American male students, especially those in adolescence. Their mantra has come to be "I'll respect him or her if they respect me." Many African American males, in particular, have felt disrespected throughout their school careers. A teacher's reaction and communication with a student can either de-escalate or escalate a discipline event. The teacher's understanding of the African American male's feelings in this regard and a respect for cultural norms of communication can go far in preventing events from escalating.

If teachers will follow the communication guidelines described, then classroom conflicts will decrease. After all, our goal is not to simply punish students but to teach them more appropriate ways in which to behave and to prevent conflict and the escalation of incidents. When students get into trouble, they are not in class or in school; each day they are not in class or in school, they fall farther behind and their chances for academic success decreases.

Use the SSS method: the first "S" is "stroke," the second "S" is "sting," and the third "S" is "stroke" again. First, say something positive about the student; next, indicate your disappointment in his behavior; and then say something positive about the student again and your hopes for behavior that is more like the person that you know that he really is or can be. This technique can get a point across while defusing a situation. Teachers who have used this method find that it works!

Go to part V and complete reflective exercises 8.1–8.4.

*Part III*

# Changing Perceptions

# NINE

## Adolescent Development

It is in adolescence that black youth are most susceptible to the destructive effects of adultification. They are deprived of their innocence and judged by adult standards of behavior. Adolescence is normally a time of tumultuous change, developing independence, questioning, and engaging in risk-taking behavior.

Black adolescents are referred, suspended, and often arrested for the errors of judgment and misbehavior that are considered normative for white youth. The goal of this chapter is to encourage educators to look through a different lens and to view black adolescents free of culturally conditioned beliefs as well as perceptions blurred by the assumptions of adultification.

Discipline referrals typically increase dramatically in middle school, especially, and high school. Teachers, administrators, and staff expect behaviors from adolescents that are outside of any normal frame of reference. Adolescence is a time of growth and maturation of the brain and, as result, the emergence of new problematic behaviors in the school setting. The prefrontal context, which is responsible for thinking logically, weighing pros and cons, and restraint, matures later. *The prefrontal cortex, the last of the brain area to mature completely, can occur as late as age thirty in all races.*

To avoid adultification, which contributes to racial disparity in referring and disciplinary actions, it is prudent to consider and remember the following about normal adolescent behavior.

The immature prefrontal cortex of the adolescent means that:

- Changes in attention, motivation, and risk-taking behaviors will occur.
- A surge in sex hormones and increase in sexual motivation will occur.
- Impulsivity, risk-taking, and reckless behaviors will be exhibited.
- Risk-taking such as showing off and disobedience is normative.
- The benefits of risk-taking outweigh the consequences.
- Less able to inhibit impulsive behavior such as fighting.
- Immediate rather than future rewards are most important.

The referral begins with the beliefs, thoughts, and feelings of the referral agent. The determination of whether an action is offensive is a subjective one governed by the following things:

- the extent to which one believes a school rule has been broken.
- the effect of the offense on other students.
- the discipline record of the student.
- the understanding of normal adolescent behavior.
- one's tolerance for that behavior.
- the color of the skin of the child committing the offense.

## BLACK ADOLESCENT DEVELOPMENT

The "Who am I?" and "Where am I going?" questions to be answered by youth in the normative identity crisis of adolescence are exacerbated for African American youth, especially males. The path to answering these questions by African American preteens and teens are complicated by issues not faced by majority youth. No majority male must be given "the talk" to save his life from the police.

African American youth have a unique and additional set of developmental tasks that they must achieve. They must master identity roles as African Americans and as members of the larger society. But the major task of African American youth is to learn how to navigate and negotiate in a racist society that defines them through a stereotypical lens.

African American males must learn to respond to perceived threats. Why do black boys run from the police? Historical and present-day experiences in person or observed of a seventeen-year old Trayvon Martin or twelve-year old Tamir Rice are racist traumas to which black boys cannot easily overcome. Part of the developmental tasks of African American males is to manage traumatic experiences and to develop the ability to self-regulate emotions around these events.

A group of high-school seniors, composed of four Hispanic females, one Hispanic male, three African American males, ten African American females, discussed the critical questions that adolescents must answer—Who am I? and Where am I going? The students self-identified as either Hispanic or African American. Their responses to questions posed follow:

"How are you viewed in this society?"

African American males:

- hostile
- stupid
- narrow-minded
- ruthless
- gangster
- dumb jock

Hispanic male

- undocumented

Hispanic females:

- inferior
- incompetent
- clueless
- undereducated

African American females:

- angry (several respondents)
- rude
- unappreciated
- incapable
- conceited
- judged
- no manners
- dysfunctional

"What obstacles might hinder you in achieving your goals?" (All indicated that they wished to attend college.)

- racial discrimination
- economic issues
- test scores
- no family/being alone
- rejection
- feeling that I can't
- no help from teachers

"What factors can help or facilitate your achieving your goals?"

- perseverance (a frequent response)
- focus
- motivation
- drive
- not doubting/confidence
- adult belief in me
- family support (the most frequent response)

Early on, African American students learn that the United States will be different for them. They understand that they will face discrimination, injustices, and even death because of the color of their skin. What they should not have to expect is that they will face racism in school, the harbor into which all children are supposed to feel cared for and safe. It was obvious that the group is aware of the role that race plays in their lives now as students and how it might affect their futures.

Go to part V and complete reflective exercises 9.1 and 9.2.

# TEN

# School Discipline and School Climate

The goal of school discipline is to create school environments that are safe and orderly so that teachers can teach and students can learn. Some school environments, however, actually work against this goal in that they promote and perpetuate discipline events. Research by Mattison and Abner (2007) indicates that positive perceptions of a school's racial climate are associated with both higher student achievement and fewer discipline problems. In this chapter, we will examine the types of school climates that promote and perpetuate rather than lessen the number of discipline events that occur.

It is important to remember that the school experience of students of color mirror those of their parents and other adults of their group in mainstream society. If African American men are feared and profiled in the larger society, then African American male students will have the same experience in the school setting. Our schools, like other institutions, mirror the beliefs held about African Americans in the American mind.

Two factors, the school *culture* and school *climate*, determine the quality of the school experiences of students from caste or involuntary minority groups. The school culture (i.e., the beliefs, values, and assumptions that guide school policies and practices) shape *the school climate* (i.e., the atmosphere or feel of the school). If the ideology of inferiority (intellectual, cultural, or moral) undergirds the belief structure about students of color, then policies and practices will reflect this ideology, resulting in a school climate that is not inviting and, in some cases, even hostile to these students.

A school's culture and climate not only can support or impede the learning process of students of color but also determines the discipline policies and practices as it relates to these students. The school culture and climate will influence how "discipline is experienced" by African American students, males, in particular. The school climate can, to a large extent, even impact student behavior, especially when it serves as a catalyst for student resentment, rebelliousness, and ultimate acting out.

The lack of understanding of the culture of African American students and culturally conditioned beliefs about African Americans, especially males, makes control the goal of discipline for African American students. This control through discipline policies and practices is applied to African American students in both predominately mainstream and predominately African American schools but may be experienced by the students in different ways.

In both cases, however, these discipline practices elicit anger, resentment, and rebelliousness from African American students. Much of the behavior described as "defiance" is a reaction to the School Powerlessness Syndrome experienced by African American students in these school environments.

## THE AFRICAN AMERICAN ADOLESCENT SCHOOL EXPERIENCE

The perceptions held of the school climate by African American students is critical to understanding their attitudes, behavior, and engagement. Research has shown that African American negative perceptions of the school climate are associated with more discipline problems among the group.

Student surveys and self-reports by African American male students indicate that they feel less supported, engaged, and safe in school. They report daily experiences of prejudice and racism. Self-reports by African American female adolescents described prejudice, discrimination, and differential treatment, as well as stereotyping, labels, and low expectations.

In terms of discipline, African American students often experience school climates as hostile. Discipline for African American students is dispensed arbitrarily, swiftly, harshly, and unfairly.

African American students most often describe feelings of being targeted and of being repeatedly sent out of class for doing little or nothing.

African American students also reported feelings of being constantly under surveillance; "She keeps her eyes on us."

What is most disheartening to hear from these students is their sense of powerlessness: "They won't listen to us, we are always wrong." Most often, it is as a result of this sense of powerlessness, the feeling of being disrespected, and their need to defend themselves in an environment in which one student described as "feeling like an outcast," and that leads to discipline events and suspensions.

There is the unfounded and misguided belief that unfair discipline practices are only a problem in predominately mainstream schools. It is assumed that in most ethnic schools that because the majority of the students are African American, the culture of these students is respected and stereotyping does not occur. Nothing could be further from the truth. Unwarranted and excessive discipline is a major problem in predominately ethnic minority schools. In view of the numbers of low achievement in such schools, it is imperative that we examine more closely the discipline policies and practices in these schools.

The same school-related factors that result in large numbers of African American students being suspended from predominately mainstream schools are operative in predominately African American schools. As was stated previously, predominately African American and Hispanic/Latino schools are most likely to have zero-tolerance policies. The climate of many predominately African American schools is authoritarian and punitive. At some level, conscious or unconscious, it is believed that the large numbers of minority and poor students make the need for such an approach to discipline absolutely necessary.

In many predominately African American schools, the attempt to control all aspects of student life and behavior is pervasive. Students describe this type of climate as "feeling like a jail." Their feelings are probably warranted in that jail terminology or jargon is part of the school lexicon; one hears of "holding cells" (where large groups of students are sequestered); "lockdown"; "death row" (a row in which all males are seated); and "repeat offender" (students who have been suspended many times).

In an extreme case, student movement is constantly monitored by not being able to go to the bathroom during the first or last thirty minutes of a ninety-minute block class and dress codes are rigidly enforced, such as students being referred for a shirt untucked, not wearing a belt, or forgetting to wear an identification badge. In this type of school climate, a general feeling of tension exists with both teachers and students expressing feelings of "we vs. them" and being in "separate camps."

For African American students, a most unfortunate consequence of this type of school environment is the lack of outlets for student involvement and leadership development. Students report that they are not allowed to engage in group work because "they are afraid that we might get out of control."

As with African American students in predominately mainstream schools, students in predominately African American schools also feel disrespected and not listened to. Many students who were interviewed and worked with expressed feelings of deep resentment about being controlled and not being trusted.

The type of atmosphere described does not promote a positive learning environment; in fact, in many ways it incites student misbehavior. The level of powerlessness produced only encourages student rebellion in the form of disobeying rules, disrespect, and defiance. This type of school climate invites, rather than lessens, the number of discipline events. The authoritarian-punitive-control–oriented schools focusing on obedience and subservience are an expression of the historical black codes that were used to govern the movement and behavior of African Americans, especially males.

Whether it is a predominately mainstream or predominately ethnic minority school, decreasing and preventing the occurrence of discipline events will require a change in the school culture and climate. Racial disparity in discipline will occur in school cultures and climates in which racialized discipline is the norm. This uncomfortable truth is a reflection of the larger problems outside of the schools.

## THE SCHOOL DISEMPOWERMENT SYNDROME

Daily racial microaggression insults, disrespect, hassles related to race trap African American students, males in particular, in a School Powerlessness Syndrome. Powerlessness is the sense that we cannot exert influence, effect change, or take control of our life situations. By law, African American students must attend school until a certain age, which means they must find methods to cope with racism within the school setting.

There are predictable feelings and behaviors that result from a sense of powerlessness. These reactions to powerlessness in the school environment may be internalized or externalized. When African American students internalize their reactions to the powerlessness felt in school, they become depressed, frustrated, anxious, helpless, and experience low self-esteem as they internalize negative stereotypes.

The most common externalized feelings are anger and resentment. Aggression is common, and students may exhibit behaviors such as distrust, defensiveness, opposition, and hypersensitivity, especially as related to respect. Lateral or horizontal violence in the form of fighting each other is common. Both male and female African American students resist and strike out in the only way in which they can when they perceive racism in any form.

When African American students perceive discrimination in school settings; they do not feel that their teachers care, and they become frustrated, lose interest, and disengage from school. Some are absent as much as possible or wait until they are old enough to drop out.

## TYPICAL CONFLICTS RELATED TO RACE AND CULTURAL VALUES

Tardiness and skipping class are often the cause of student referrals. Time issues are relevant as related to the culture of African American students and can best be dealt within teachable moments rather than referrals.

The rigid use of time is a mainstream (European) American value. According to Althen (1988), Americans regard time as a resource "time is money." The ideal person in this society, in a cultural sense, is one who is punctual and considerate of other's time.

Althen (1988) concedes that this attitude toward time is not necessarily shared by non-Europeans, who regard time as something around them rather than something to use. He states that one of the most difficult adjustments that many foreign businessmen and students must make in the United States is the notion that time must be saved whenever possible and "used" wisely every day.

The African American relationship to and concept of time has been problematic for them in this country since the enslavement period. According to Sobel (1987), "the use of time was at the heart of owners' criticism of slaves: they wanted slaves to change their perception of time and work."

Time continues to cause problems for African American students. The concept of social time adhered to by many African American students causes them to be chronically late to school or class. It is important, however, for the teacher to distinguish between two groups of tardy students.

"Adjustors" (who are adjusting time to fit their social definition) move along slowly, chatting with each other, and enjoying the moment when going to school or class. They are caught up in the moment and regard the social situation as more important than the schedule. With "avoiders," the focus of being late is to avoid unpleasantness, either because they are unable to perform adequately or because they expect to have conflict with the teacher.

## DEALING WITH TIME ISSUES

1. Realize that the concept of time enforced at school is only one group's way of relating to time. Like other aspects of deep culture, the way one relates to time influences one's view of the world and how to operate in it.
2. Have a dialogue with students about the ways different cultures regard time. Point out that the school culture requires that all students adhere to a rigid time schedule. Explain why punctuality is necessary in the school setting.
3. Allow students to brainstorm ways to incorporate flexibility in the classroom time schedule.
4. Talk to chronically late students; find out why they are late and determine if they are adjustors or avoiders. Use different strategies with each type of student; remember that being late to class is a symptom of a much larger problem for the avoider.
5. Be aware that some conflicts that occur in the classroom may be a rebellion against the rigid adherence to time.
6. Be as flexible as possible with schedules.
7. Give ample warning when changing from one activity to another.
8. Provide sufficient "wait time" for students to respond to questions (at least five seconds); African American males have a tendency to respond more slowly because they want to be absolutely sure of their response.

## JUSTICE

A value held by African American students that causes problems in the classroom is the need for fairness, equality, and justice. African American students are keenly aware of unfairness; they are always vigilant and analyze situations to determine if injustice has occurred. In this respect, African American males have a great need to be heard and to explain their side.

Most often, conflicts occur and incidents escalate because the African American male student feels that he was not taken seriously, was not listened to, or was not given the opportunity to tell his side. When any of these three events occurs, the African American male will persist in talking to be heard or to state his case.

Unless the teacher listens, this situation will build to a point where the student (in the words of African American male students) "snaps" or "goes off on the teacher." Many African American male students feel that this is the only way that they can get a teacher to really listen to them.

## TEN WAYS TO DECREASE CONFLICTS RELATED TO CULTURAL DIFFERENCES IN THE CLASSROOM

1. Realize that the denial and devaluation of the culture of African American students is cultural racism (see Lustig and Koester 1996).
2. Ask: "What works in a culturally diverse school environment so that the norms of all ethnic groups are to some extent acknowledged and respected?"
3. Facilitate dialogues on cultural attributes and identity so that students can distinguish between traditional positive cultural practices (collectivism) from negative cultural practices, such as wearing of pants with no belts (from the prison culture).
4. Facilitate dialogues that distinguish between stereotypes, which originate outside the group and are used to control the group, and cultural attributes, which come from the group itself and are used to meet the needs of the group.
5. Do not be quick to accuse students of cheating; you may be seeing an innocent display of cooperation.
6. Let students help determine classroom rules and school discipline codes.

7. Always leave room for negotiation.
8. Seek input from parents and individuals from the community regarding the issue of cultural differences and discipline.
9. Refrain from assuming that all the negative behaviors exhibited by African American students are aspects of traditional African American culture; they are usually merely adolescent behaviors, no matter the ethnicity.
10. Incorporate collectivistic values and practices in the classroom, such as peer tutoring, cooperative learning activities, and whole-class teaching.

A major problem occurs when teachers and administrators view African American students through the lens of institutional racism that black students are facing in their school. These teachers and administrators are unaware of the unconscious racism that these students face on a daily basis. Teachers will mistake depression as having an attitude or defiance; they will see students as aggressive, never understanding the anger and, sometimes, rage that has built up in them as a result of their school experience.

This brings us to a crucial aspect of analyzing the "discipline event." We must ask "Why?" Why is this black student so angry, so defensive? What has happened to make him or her this way? When the "Why" is never asked, we punish students when we need to be showing them that we understand and that we care.

For instance, a tall, dark, quiet young man did his work but kept mostly to himself, although he did socialize with the guys. He would be fine for weeks, and then some days, he would come in angry with the world. He would immediately be thrown out of class. Not once after five or six suspensions did anyone, teacher, or administrator, ask "Why?" The author who was working with what are often called in school jargon "high fliers" (i.e., those with repeated suspensions), asked him what happens when he comes to school so upset. He trusted the author enough to divulge that he was fine until he would see his father who would not recognize him as his son. He would be hurt and angry for days.

This young man should have been seeing a counselor to help him cope with this hurtful situation rather than being excluded from school. Perhaps at some point, the counselor or administrator could have reached out to his father to try to remedy the situation. This hurting adolescent was only seen as a violent troublemaker, a thug; he had no humanity to the teacher or the administrator.

One of the most damaging effects of cultural conditioning is the impact that it has on the victim. When black students internalize the negative stereotypes, they act out in ways that become a self-fulfilling prophecy and confirm the culturally conditioned beliefs in the eyes of the teacher. When one seventh grader was asked why he was clowning around and acting up, he insisted that this was the way that he [a black male] was supposed to act. Rather than automatically assuming he was a troublemaker, a "Why?" might have provided insight into the student's behavior.

Because young black males see that black adult males get no respect in this society, they are hypervigilant about being respected. A slight of any sort, even an accidental brushing up against a young black man, can end in a fight. The punishment for fighting, no matter who the initiator, appears to be suspension or if an officer is available, arrest.

This form of horizontal violence should be met with conflict resolution and engagement in a "critical conversation" about what it means to be a black man in this society and how one earns respect. Again, because we as educators only see the stereotypical Brute, we do not ask "Why?"

We must see African American students through a different lens, free of the culturally conditioned beliefs and images that are held of them. We should also attempt to see more clearly what the daily experience of young black adolescents is like in the school setting. Finally, a sense of empathy must be developed for the young black adolescents who struggle to discover who they are and what they can hope for in the future.

One of the most effective ways to reduce disciplinary events in the classroom is to establish authentic relationships with African American students, especially males. Because of the pervasiveness of stereotyping, African American males are the most intimidating and feared of all students. It is African American male students who need relationships with teachers most, but they are the least likely to have those relationships.

A series of critical conversations with male students in a predominately African American high school was revealing. The males were suspicious and slow to warm. As African American males progress through the grades, they sense that they are treated differently and unfairly; their anger and resentment toward the "system" grows. By the time they reach secondary school, many are so distrustful that it takes great effort to reach them.

A major turning point in the conversations came when the session focused on stereotyping. Some boys who had been reserved opened up, and some who had previously played around took an interest in the session. In fact, they rated the session on stereotyping as the best session. What appeared to have happened was that for the first time, these young men recognized that an adult was sincerely interested in them and understood what they endured being African American males. One of the things that African American males need most is to feel that they are listened to and understood.

To start the relationship-building process with African American male students:

- Try to really understand what it is like to live under the yoke of negative stereotyping.
- Recognize that much of their anger and resentment (displayed as "defiant" behavior) comes from the knowledge that they have been, are, and will be treated differently in this society.
- Engage them in a conversation about what it means to them to be an African American male.
- Really listen to them; not only their words but their feelings.
- Take a personal interest in them.
- Take an interest in the "whole" person and not just academics.
- Explore with him his talents and abilities.
- Constantly verbalize your high expectations for him.
- Let them know through your actions toward them that you do not believe the stereotypes about African American males.

Poverty, family problems, low academic skills, and personal issues can and do precipitate student acting out. You can lessen the extent to which these events occur and escalate in your classroom by building relationships with your African American students.

The same approaches described in this book to eliminate racial disparities in discipline, as they pertain to African American students, can be adapted for use in schools with predominately Hispanic/Latino and American Indian populations.

Go to part V and complete reflective exercises 10.1–10.4.

# ELEVEN
## The Disciplinary Event Analysis

Changes in discipline practices can only occur if changes are made at the individual level. All discipline events begin at an interpersonal level. Primarily two adults, the teacher or staff member and the administrator make a determination if a student's behavior merits a referral and what the punishment should be for the misbehavior according to school rules.

The teacher or staff member at a subjective level (unless the offense involves weapons, drugs, bullying, or assault) perceives an action to be offensive or in violation of school rules and writes a referral. After reviewing the referral, the administrator also makes a subjective judgment about what the punishment should be for the offense.

The Reflective Discipline process requires that the following set of questions be asked and reflected on before a referral is written:

- What was the perceived infraction?
- When did the perceived infraction occur?
- Who committed the perceived infraction?
- Why did the perceived infraction occur?
- What is the best way to make this a teachable moment for the student perceived to have committed the infraction?

These questions are crucial to avoiding racial profiling and disparity in discipline.

1. *What* was the perceived offense?

- Because the majority of referrals are for minor offenses, the teacher or staff must be certain that the perceived offense is such that a referral is necessary.
- Was the act meant to be hurtful or normative adolescent misbehavior?
- What feelings were attached to my thoughts about the incident?

2. *When* did the infraction occur?

- Under what conditions did the perceived infraction occur?
- Was a response required of the offending student?
- Did the student perceive the teacher's comments as a microaggression?
- Was the class in transition?

3. *Who* was the offending party?

- Male? Female? It is extremely important, especially based on the reflection work we have done so far with culturally conditioned beliefs and images that the teacher's perception is not blurred by stereotypical images.
- Did we see an adolescent or an adultification of an adult black male or female commit the offense?

4. *Why* is the most important question that we must ask before writing a referral.

- Why did the student commit the infraction?
- Was this a ruse to escape having to perform in class?
- Was the student attempting to get attention and approval from peers?
- Was the student's response a reaction to the "Student Powerlessness Syndrome?"
- Was anger and aggression attached to the student's response?

5. *How* can we turn this event into a teachable moment?

- Is conflict management, problem solving, anger management, counseling, or a critical conversation between teacher and student the best way to prevent the reoccurrence of the behavior?
- Is this an occasion for a class critical conversation about race, feelings of powerlessness, stereotyping, the impact of internalized stereotyping, and so on?

The teacher should be able to answer each of these questions appropriately before writing the referral, and the administrator must be able to answer the same questions before deciding on the most suitable response that will promote adolescent development. Because discipline problems occur between individuals, the event must be examined at the micro or interpersonal level.

## WHAT, WHEN, AND WHERE TO REFER

Powerful teachers express pride that they make few referrals to the office because "I can handle my problems myself in the classroom." One reason that "they take care of their own problems" is that they feel it is part of "good teaching." Second, they do not want to convey the message to the student that they are unable to handle them. Third, they will say that they have learned from experience that whoever disciplines the student is the adult who earns the student's respect, and they refuse to give away their power.

One aspect of good classroom management is learning what, when, and where to refer students when inappropriate behavior occurs in the classroom. Two guidelines that teachers with good classroom management follow are:

- Remember that all human behavior is goal directed; there is some need that the student who is acting out is trying to meet. Ask yourself: "Why is this student acting out? Why is this student frustrated in this class?"
- A referral should always assist the student in some way to change his or her behavior; therefore, even discipline should be more than simply punishment. In an educational setting, there must be an educational component as well. Ask yourself: "How will this referral help the student to change his or her behavior?"

Glasser (1986) posits that still another question be asked: "What can the teacher do to help the disruptive student find the class more satisfying?" He suggests that only a discipline program that is also concerned with classroom satisfaction will work.

Some years ago, a Superintendent's Advisory Committee developed a Cultural Awareness Guide for all current and incoming teachers. One of the major issues that the district was addressing was racial disparity in

discipline. Tables 11.1 and 11.2 were developed by the Discipline and
Classroom Management Writing Team. These exercises are for you, the
reader. Reflect and answer the questions on the self-evaluation as honestly as possible.

Do not be afraid of seeing areas in which you need to improve or
develop; a conscious awareness of your relationship issues with African
American students is key to correcting these issues and decreasing conflicts with African American students. The do's and don'ts presented in
Table 11.2 are excellent techniques for decreasing tension, conflicts, and
discipline referrals.

"Exceptional" teachers, counselors, and social workers who are also
peer facilitators described student behaviors in terms of four categories of
teacher responses: incidents to ignore, incidents in which the teacher
would take advantage of a teachable moment, incidents that provided the
teacher an opportunity to examine his classroom management style, and
incidents that required a referral of some type. The referrals were of six
types: counselor, parent, peer, Student Support Team, adult mentor, and
administrator. Some incidents did not warrant giving the student the
power to draw attention away from teaching the class; if the behavior
persisted, and was truly disruptive for the class, then it would be dealt
with. They felt that teaching is part of disciplining and that some incidents would not occur again or would lessen if students were taught why
they were inappropriate. The teachers also felt that some number of incidents could be prevented if the teacher used more effective classroom
management skills. As you will see in Table 11.1, these "exceptional" and
"seasoned" teachers referred only the most serious offenses to an administrator.

## GIVING UP THE NEED TO CONTROL

The one thing that was central to the discipline practices of these teachers–facilitators was that they had no sense of a need to "control" their
students. They believed that they should focus on "good teaching"—
challenging, hands-on activities to keep students involved, so that they
did not have time for excesses; cooperative learning and peer tutoring
that allowed "structured socialization," so that students did not feel con-
strained and deprived of peer contact; and most importantly, letting eve-

Table 11.1 What, When, and Where to Refer

| *Incidents to Ignore* | *Incidents to Take Advantage of the Teachable Moment* |
|---|---|
| Habits (e.g., sitting on legs, rocking in desk, chewing on pencil, shaking legs, tapping) | Not wanting to play or work with others |
| Noisy hair beads | Student says "I can't do this" |
| Passing notes | Ridiculing another child's clothing or work |
| Shirttail out | Teasing other students |
| Pitching paper into trash | Tattling |
| Chewing gum | Using inappropriate nonprofanity (e.g., "frigging, sucks, crap, freaking") |
| Tapping another student | Talking or laughing when another student is talking |
| Nonverbal language: rolling eyes, popping lips | Anger (count to ten) |
| | Not wanting to play together |

| *Incidents to Examine Classroom* | *Incidents Requiring a Referral* |
|---|---|
| Classroom management style | *To a counselor:* |
| Excessive talking | Bullying |
| Sleeping students | Stealing |
| Tardies | Fighting |
| Not bringing materials to class | *To a parent:* |
| Requests to go to bathroom | Stealing |
| Students begin to converse after extended lecture (may need a break) | Bad language |
| Sharpening pencil (inappropriate time) | Doesn't complete assignments |
| Getting out of/remaining in desk | Fighting |
| Name-calling | *To an adult mentor:* |
| Picking on others | Apathy (academics) |
| | Doesn't complete assignments |

| *Incidents Requiring Referral to Student Support Team* | |
|---|---|
| *Administrator* | *To a peer:* |
| Fighting | Apathy (academics) |
| Weapons | Behavior (better behaved student) |
| | Academics (peer tutor) |

Threats

Defiant behavior

Sexual harassment

---

ry student know that the teacher expected them to learn because the teacher had the ability to teach them.

The need to control always comes from a sense of fear—fear of our own inadequacies or fear of the students that we are assigned to teach. Most fear of the students we teach comes from culturally conditioned beliefs; for example, they are undisciplined, aggressive, violent, out of control, and prone to riot, etc. There tends to be a long-standing, deep-seated historical fear of African Americans, especially males, in groups, whether it is on street corners, in school hallways, or classrooms. We rarely fear white, upper-class males, even though this group of students has committed our greatest school tragedies.

When low expectations for behavior and fear are communicated to students, they intuitively sense a teacher's fear and will test your resolve at every turn. They will also resent the fearful teacher because they are angered by the teacher's perception of them. The best rule to probably follow is to never teach a group of students that you fear. It is more productive for both you and the students if you teach those students with whom you are comfortable.

Dealing with fear issues and giving up the need to control African American students will be a great step toward decreasing tension in the classroom and improving relationships with African American students. This in no way implies that there should not be rules and expectations for appropriate behavior.

It is ironic that the best teachers are also the "toughest," in the sense that they have rules that they expect students to follow, not to control them but to make the classroom run more efficiently. They do not fear students, and they feel no need to control students. Most importantly, they refuse to give their power away. These teachers trust their students to meet the high expectations they hold for them, they are always teaching in social as well as classroom situations, and they trust their power to teach and make a difference in the lives of all students with whom they come in contact.

## CULTURAL SENSITIVITY AND CLASSROOM MANAGEMENT

Acquiring accurate information about the cultural attributes of African American students, acknowledging and appreciating the differences between African American and European-based mainstream culture, and practicing the cultural etiquette can be helpful to the teacher in classroom management.

At the heart of the matter is a simple equation: balancing the relationship that exists between African American students and their teachers. The quality of that relationship will determine if communication and rapport, or tension and conflict, occurs between them. Faulty assumptions, erroneous beliefs, and fear that results from historical stereotypes will block the development of a healthy relationship between teacher and student. A lack of knowledge and understanding of the culture of African American students will interfere with the creation of effective communication between the teacher and student.

Table 11.2. Culturally Effective and Ineffective Classroom Management Techniques

| DO'S | DON'TS |
| --- | --- |
| Allow student to have time out after disciplinary action has been taken | Have too many rules |
| Allow students point of view to be heard | Get in the face of a student (sign of aggression) |
| Use "teachable moments" | Yell |
| Keep your "cool" | Demand eye contact |
| Post reasonable rules | Touch (in a situation with anger) |
| Refer problem students to counselor | Demand student to use "yes, ma'am" or "yes, sir" |
| Be willing to try counselor's strategies | Call students "boy" or "girl" |
| Be aware of your own baggage (e.g., having a bad day or argument with spouse) | Make situations a power struggle |
| Be consistent | Deny students their right to be heard |
| Realize you are not perfect | Take it personally |
| Be willing to say you are sorry | Expect submissiveness (threatening) |
| | Allow/encourage hearsay (mutual respect) |

Go to part V and complete reflective exercises 11.1 and 11.2.

*Part IV*

# A New Perspective

# TWELVE

# Reflective Discipline: The Leader's Role

Although the Reflective Discipline model is essentially an individualized approach to eliminating racial profiling in discipline, it is the role and responsibility of the school leader to ensure that the process is successful. The leader must embrace the concept and model the behavior of one who "sees" African American students differently.

## THE LEADER'S ROLE

The principal's attitude and commitment to creating an accessible, equitable, and culturally sensitive school environment is the most important element in bringing about the needed changes. The leader must set the tone, initiate the process, guide the process, and hold teachers and staff accountable for creating a classroom environment in which all students feel respected and treated fairly. Ultimately, the principal has the responsibility for ensuring the elimination of any factors that place African American students at risk for unnecessary and unfair disciplinary referrals. The principal will provide the leadership necessary to ensure the collective success of the Reflective Discipline process.

The principal must model the values of Reflective Discipline, provide needed information to increase teacher competency, and coach those teachers who are uncomfortable or resistant to the process. Finally, the principal must set the standards for professional ethics and establish the criteria for evaluation as it pertains to engagement in the process.

The principal must provide leadership in three key areas initiating the process, guiding the process, and evaluating the process.

## INITIATING THE CHANGE PROCESS

In the initiation phase of the process, the principal must determine the faculty and staff's

- attitudes toward African American students.
- perceptions of the need to specifically address issues related to African American students.
- openness to participate in the process.
- level of support that is needed to make the process successful.
- sense of buy in or ownership of the process.

### *Step 1: Assessing Faculty Attitudes toward African American Students*

The attitudes held toward African American students by faculty and staff members will, to a large extent, determine the faculty's perception of the need to examine school-related factors that may lead to disparities in the disciplinary process. The first task of the principal, therefore, is to make some determination about the attitudes held toward African American students.

This can be done in two ways: by conducting an informal climate audit and through dialogues with faculty members. Because beliefs precede behaviors, the best way to get a feel for teacher attitudes toward African American students is to observe interactions between teachers and students in classrooms and other campus settings. The purpose of the observations and the dialogues is to help the principal determine the beliefs that are held about, and the feelings toward, African American students.

At this point, the principal should also be interested in determining the extent to which faculty and staff members understand or feel that they understand the culture of African American students. Finally, it is important to see the type and quality of interactions between African American students and their teachers.

A point of departure for the dialogues may simply be, "We seem to be experiencing a number of disciplinary problems with our African American students. What do you feel is the cause of these problems?" It is important at this point for the principal to create a climate in which faculty members feel free to express their beliefs and feelings toward the students.

To eliminate the school-related at-risk factors for African American students, changes will have to occur in the faculty's belief system regarding African Americans, feelings toward African Americans, level of knowledge about the culture of African Americans, and interactions with and behaviors toward African American students.

*Step 2: Establishing the Need for Change*

Reflective Discipline is a new concept, one that places the responsibility for confronting, challenging, and changing beliefs on the individual. Many faculty and staff members will find this process uncomfortable because it requires them to take an intimate look at race. It is important that the principal explain that this is not about placing blame or having individuals feel shame, but rather a process to free one of any beliefs that might interfere with them being the professional that needs to work with all students well.

In a school setting, where the majority of students are not African American, there might be complaints about the focus of the process being African American students. Often the feeling is that they should be concerned about all of the students rather than focusing on this group of students. In this case, the principal has to establish or indicate the need to focus on African American students.

To help establish a need, the principal has to rely on the school's statistical data, disaggregated by race, gender, and social class, if possible. By using this type of data, a picture will emerge that clearly shows the group of students that presents the most critical need for attention. It is important to reveal the findings of national studies that show that race is the most significant factor in determining who gets referred and for what reasons.

Conducting separate focus groups with teachers, students, and parents can provide insights that will support the need to focus on the issues related to African American students and discipline. At one parent forum that focused only on the issue of discipline, sixty-five African American parents attended. School officials were amazed because they had previously had little success in getting African American parents to attend meetings. The attendance of these parents decried the myth that African American parents do not care about their children's education.

These parents were concerned about what was happening to their children, and disparity in discipline was a major concern. Also, to the surprise of the school officials, these African American parents did want their children disciplined. They, however, wanted discipline to be administered in a fair and consistent manner. One attitude to take is that, "If there is a perception of a problem, then there is a problem." African American parents are starting to voice many concerns and to seek redress in the courts for issues related to disparities in discipline.

Although many faculty members may not be as inclined to hear the opinions of students regarding why they misbehave and the disciplinary process in general, it is recommended that input be solicited from students as well. (Student perceptions of disciplinary issues and school climate are located in part 5.) It is important to hear from the students who are experiencing the most problems in the area of discipline.

*Step 3: Motivating the Faculty to Be Open to the Process*

To reduce disproportionality in disciplinary referrals and to eliminate school-related factors that contribute to the problem, the faculty must be willing to participate in the process. A combination of the "stick-and-carrot" approach appears to be work best.

The carrot in learning how to better understand and relate to African American student is that it will simply make life easier for the teacher. Cross-cultural interactions can be stressful if one does not understand or appreciate cultural differences. Holding stereotypes, even unconscious ones, produces stress in the form of fear and the feeling that one has to constantly maintain some sense of control when interacting with the stereotyped individual.

Adopting culturally responsive and responsible behaviors will reduce teacher stress, promote better relationships with African American students, and add to teaching effectiveness. From a basically selfish point of view, teaching African American students will become infinitely easier if the teacher actively engages in this process. Academic performance will improve as well as classroom performance. In this age of grading teachers and schools as well as students, less class time lost to suspensions will enhance student, teacher, and school grades.

From the point of view of teacher accountability and professional standards, teachers have an ethical responsibility to learn how to teach all students well. Releasing old culturally conditioned beliefs and learning accurate information is part of our professional responsibility and also the key to our professional empowerment.

The new teaching reality requires that teacher evaluations and promotions consider culturally responsive and responsible behavior as part of the evaluation criteria. The principal must in no uncertain terms make it clear that in this school environment, teacher effectiveness includes the willingness to grow as a teacher (actively participate in the Reflective Discipline process) and the demonstration of culturally responsive behaviors.

*Step 4: Support the Development of New Competencies*

Professional development in the form of training related to African American culture and African American adolescent development and identity issues must be provided for the faculty. The lack of accurate information about African American culture and African American students, male and female, is a major contributor to the problems that occur between African American students and their teachers. The Reflective Discipline process provides a method for learning critical competencies to change discipline dynamics in a school.

Instituting a buddy system by matching teachers who have problems with teachers who are most effective in teaching African American students and who have few discipline problems with these students can be beneficial. There is always at least one teacher who can establish a relationship with the most troubled student. Have the teachers who are experiencing the most problems (the most referrals) seek advice from and observe the more effective teachers.

It is important for the principal to emphasize again and again that the Reflective Discipline process is not intended as teacher bashing; it is a way to help teachers find ways to be more effective in reducing tension and conflict between themselves and African American students.

*Step 5: Promoting Ownership of the Process*

This process is intended to change the school culture. As such, it requires not only the active participation of the faculty and staff but also their buy in and ownership of the process. Eliminating the school-related factors that contribute to these disciplinary referrals and actions must also be a school goal. It is imperative that this process become a school-wide project, using the Reflective Discipline process to systematically bring about change. Although the principal has the responsibility for initiating and guiding the process, all members of the school community must be included in the process: teachers, staff, SROs, students, parents, and interested community leaders.

## ENSURING EQUITY THROUGH CHANGES IN POLICIES AND PROCEDURES

Eliminating school-related factors that lead to disparities in the disciplinary process require that changes occur at the policy and procedure levels. This process will be initiated by the principal and implemented through the involvement of teachers, parents, students, and individuals from the community.

Suggested ways to make changes in policies and procedures that will promote culturally responsive and responsible behaviors related to the issue of discipline follow.

1. Form a committee made up of teachers, students, parents, and community members to review the current student disciplinary policies and procedures.
2. Make revisions in policies where necessary to ensure that there is no possibility for vague interpretations, abuse, or disparate treatment.
3. Clearly define the criteria for offense categories. What is considered disruptive, disrespectful, defiant, argumentative, or verbally aggressive behavior depends a great deal on subjective or individual interpretation. Come to clear and consistent interpretation that leaves no room for unfairness.
4. Base assessment of punishment on objective criteria. Leave no room for excessive or retaliatory punishment.
5. Clearly define how disciplinary sanctions will be imposed for specific offenses.
6. Make the examination of precipitating factors or events a part of the disciplinary process. It is important to rule out any instance of harassing or provocative behavior on the part of the teacher.

7. Allow input from a number of individuals before the imposition of serious sanctions (e.g., long-term suspensions, expulsions, or placement in an alternative school setting).
8. Any deviations from the established student disciplinary policies and procedures must be documented and approved by the committee that reviewed student disciplinary policies.
9. Establish policies and disciplinary penalties for racial harassment if none are in place.
10. Implement a procedure for providing conflict resolution training for teachers, and establish criteria for the participation of the teacher and student in the conflict resolution process.
11. Establish a procedure for assisting teachers who make an excessive number of referrals for offenses that could be handled in the classroom.
12. Establish a procedure for investigating allegations of racism, classism, and other abuses of power.

Two additional changes must occur if school-related risk factors are to be eliminated. First, the importance of establishing good teacher–student relationships must be emphasized. The quality of the teacher–student relationship will determine the effectiveness of that interaction. It is also important to remember that African American students are socialized in a collective culture. Social relationships are important and that includes the student's relationship with his teacher. When teachers have good relationships with African American students, discipline is less of a problem.

Second, the stated and unstated emphasis in the school setting must be on academics rather than discipline. There is a distinctive difference in the feel of schools whose focus is academics compared with those schools whose focus is control and discipline.

In many cases, schools with a predominately African American or low-income student population emphasize discipline rather than academics. Schools with predominately students of color and lower-income populations have more information on bulletin boards relating to following the rules and building acceptable character. On the other hand, bulletin boards in the schools that emphasized academics were devoted to content areas of the curriculum and providing new information. It appears, at least from the informal curriculum in many schools, that minority, especially poor African American students, spend more time in improving their character and learning to follow rules than focusing on academics. It is ironic, however, that in schools where the emphasis is on good teaching, with high expectations for student success, discipline tends to be less of an issue. As the beat for more police includes patrolling schools, it appears that social control of African American students rather than academic engagement, reminiscent of the early periods of African American life in the United States has returned.

## SCHOOL RESOURCE OFFICERS

Police in schools do not make African American students feel safe and protected, rather these students are intimidated, anxious, and afraid. Predominately poor African American schools with metal detectors and other surveillance equipment have the feel of prisons. It is the principal's role to make clear the responsibilities the SROs will have in the school.

SROs are law enforcement officers, who are trained to be hypervigilant, to look for anomalies and to seek out those breaking the law. SROs should only be involved in criminal investigations on school campuses. Students possessing drugs, weapons, bullying, or those considered a danger to themselves or others should be referred to SROs.

Talking back to a teacher, using profane language, disrupting a class, or violating a dress code are not criminal offenses. It is the responsibility of the principal to inform faculty and staff of the role of SROs and clearly differentiate student misbehavior from criminal offenses. The principal must examine all law enforcement referrals and scrutinize any and all racial disparity in law enforcement referrals.

The principal as school leader committed to eliminating racial profiling in school discipline and dismantling the school-to-prison pipeline must insist that any SROs patrolling the campus engage in the Reflective Discipline process. It is crucial that SROs examine the culturally conditioned beliefs they hold as a result of those held by the larger society and those learned in the academy and on the streets as well.

If SROs are to relate to African American students, it is critical that they have accurate knowledge of African American culture and the unique social tasks faced especially by African American males. The principal should require SROs to report all interactions with students and promote building positive relationships with African American students.

The principal should be clear in having teachers, staff, and SROs understand that discipline is a school-related issue that seeks developmentally and educationally appropriate solutions for student misbehavior. Critical conversations, conflict resolutions, and problem solving as well as other best practices will be employed to correct student behavior.

Go to part V and complete reflective exercise 12.1.

# THIRTEEN

# The Village Approach: Forming Partnerships with Parents and Community

The Reflective Discipline process is designed to have the teacher, administrator, staff, and SROs view the African American student through a different lens or way of seeing. It is essential that parents and communities have a role and responsibility in the process as well.

Research has indicated that African American students who are knowledgeable and grounded in their true cultural heritage are best able to cope with racism.

In this book, the role and responsibility of the school in eliminating racial disparities in discipline has been discussed. The research cited from self-reports primarily from African American students and discussions with parents, teachers, administrators, and community members indicate that significant changes must be made in beliefs, attitudes, policies, and practices within the school setting if racial disparities in discipline are to be eliminated.

When African American students are asked how their parent(s) reacted to their suspension(s), the results are sometimes amazing. They usually respond that the parent gets upset, maybe even angry, but when they are quizzed more about parental sanctions, grounding, withdrawal of privileges, and so on, there are usually none. Two things might be inferred from this seemingly apathetic behavior. One, it may be assumed that the parent just does not care about the child's misbehavior; it may be taken as an indication of a sense of powerlessness on the part of parents to impact school discipline policies.

One other possibility, however, is that the deep sense of distrust that now exists between African American parents toward the school may impact their response or lack of response. When asked how his parents reacted to his out-of-school suspension, one African American student reported his grandfather's response; "You got to watch some of those teachers; they try to get you in trouble, [they] don't want to see you go anywhere in life."

There is a definite role that African American parents and community members must play in reducing disciplinary incidents and referrals among African American students. Educators need to ask the assistance of a core group of parents and community members in addressing the problem of disparity in discipline. It will be important to include adversaries and supporters from all income strata.

A starting point might be to have parents and community members talk about their experiences in our schools, especially the way in which they experienced discipline policies and practices when they were students themselves. If these adults have had negative experiences in our schools because of cultural insensitivity, then we will necessarily have to build trust within the family for it to work with the child. Parents and community members must believe that their children will be treated fairly if they are to become our partners in resolving the problem.

## FORMING A SCHOOL–COMMUNITY PARTNERSHIP

The first step in the process is to clarify the school's role and responsibility:

1. Ask for the assistance of the community in resolving the problem.
2. Acknowledge that there is a problem of racial disparity in discipline.
3. Acknowledge that the lack of cultural knowledge and unconscious stereotyping is a factor.
4. Make a commitment to take responsibility for changing the school climate.

Secondly, clarify the community's role and responsibility.

1. Express the expectation that the community will assist.

2. Try to involve ministers and express the desire that they take a leadership role in the process.
3. Express the expectation that knowledgeable community members will take a leadership role if it is difficult to recruit parents.
4. Expect ministers and community members to influence parents to be a part of the process.

Third, ask parents and community members to:

1. Provide mentors for troubled students.
2. Serve on a task force to design discipline policies.
3. Serve on a task force to develop criteria for placement in alternative programs.
4. Serve as members of a support team for students with discipline problems.
5. Serve on committees to define disciplinary offenses.
6. Serve on hearing panels for serious offenses.
7. Conduct classes for students related to traditional African American beliefs and values.

Finally, conduct dialogues with parents and community members about:

1. Their feelings related to race, racism, and bad experiences as a student.
2. Conflicts in parent and school values. For instance, fighting at school, even to defend oneself, is a punishable offense. Many African American parents, however, insist that their children "hit back" when hit. The child may even get into trouble at home for not defending himself. Many African American parents are authoritarian in their childrearing and believe in corporal punishment (i.e., spanking or "whipping"). Some African American parents feel that their rights as a parent to discipline their children in a way that they feel is best have been taken away.
3. Provide information to:

   a. Parents and community members about the process for filing complaints or grievances.
   b. Teachers and administrators about African American culture and the issues that African American males face.

4. Provide support to:

    a. Single mothers and grandmothers raising children alone.

    b. Community groups who are willing to sponsor community-run programs for students with serious behavior problems. The strategies will be helpful in forming a partnership with parents and the community that will help increase communication, build trust, and provide a cooperative effort to decrease discipline problems.

We have examined data, school-related factors related to disparity in discipline (i.e., cultural conflict and stereotypes), and school climate. We have discussed the role that administrators, individual teachers, parents, and community can play in the process of reducing disciplinary events and suspensions. Finally, in the next chapter, we evaluate the process.

Go to part V and complete reflective exercise 13.1.

# FOURTEEN

## Evaluating the Process: School Climate and Individual Assessment

How do you know that the Reflective Discipline process in which you have engaged to eliminate school-related factors that place African American students at risk for disciplinary referrals and action is working? The most effective test is that you will see a decrease in the number of disciplinary referrals for African American students; if you are in a predominately African American school setting, you will see a decrease in disciplinary referrals in general. A by-product of this process can also be that you will have fewer complaints voiced and filed by African American parents.

Creating an environment that is characterized by an absence of racial microaggressions, and culturally responsive behaviors is an ongoing process that will not only produce significant differences in the area of discipline but will also influence the total school environment.

Evaluating the effectiveness of the change process involves conducting assessments at both the school climate and individual level. The first set of questions that follows involves an assessment of the school climate. The questions relate not only to the disciplinary process but also to all aspects of the school culture. The questions will refer to "African American students"; if your school has a majority African American student population, if appropriate you may rephrase the question to read, "African American students from lower socioeconomic backgrounds."

## SCHOOL CLIMATE ASSESSMENT

Answer "yes" or "no" to each item. If you answer "yes" to an item, give specific examples to support your response.

1. Are high expectations (academic performance and social behavior) held for African American students?
2. Do African American students feel respected and accepted in the school environment?
3. Do African American students feel a sense of connectedness to the school community?
4. Is the language and culture of African American students respected and valued?
5. Are African American students free to express their cultural identity?
6. Do the formal and informal curricula include the accomplishments and contributions of Africans and African Americans?
7. Is creating a culturally sensitive and responsive school environment a school goal?
8. Is reducing the number of disciplinary referrals involving African American students, especially males, a priority?
9. Are disciplinary referrals for African American students, especially African American males, proportionate to their numbers in the school population?
10. Has a diverse committee (e.g., race, ethnicity, social class, teachers, students, parents, community members) been established to periodically review discipline policies and issues?
11. Have discipline policies and procedures been established that eliminate disparity related to race, gender, and social class?
12. Is disaggregated data (e.g., race, gender, social class) related to academic performance and discipline reviewed periodically?
13. Do instructional and resource materials have African American representation?
14. Does a representative number of African American students participate in all types of extracurricular activities?
15. Does a representative number of African American students hold leadership positions in student government and organizations?

16. Are African American students represented in all academic levels (e.g., gifted, honors, and so on) in proportion to their numbers in the school population?

17. Do teaching styles and assessment procedures reflect an understanding of the culture and experiences of African American students?

18. Do African American parents feel comfortable and welcome in the school?

19. Is the faculty comfortable interacting with African American parents?

20. Is the school's stated emphasis one of academic achievement rather than discipline and control?

21. Does discipline focus on teaching appropriate behavior as well as punishment?

22. Are all allegations of racism, sexism, and classism investigated?

23. Is ongoing professional development and technical assistance provided for faculty and staff related to cultural differences, stereotyping, discipline, etc.?

24. Is coaching provided for faculty members who have persistent problems with African American students?

25. Is coaching provided for faculty members who are resistant to the process of becoming more culturally responsive and responsible?

26. Is coaching provided for faculty members who receive a disproportionate number of persistent complaints from students and parents?

27. Are there sanctions against negative "lounge talk" about students?

28. Are culturally responsive and responsible behaviors included in the criteria for faculty evaluations and accountability?

29. Is hiring more African American and other faculty members of color a priority?

30. Is the climate assessment an ongoing process?

## INDIVIDUAL ASSESSMENT

An assessment at the individual level will help teachers and administrators to know how they are progressing in terms of the process of culturally conditioned beliefs and becoming more culturally responsible. As was the case with the assessment of the school climate, affirmative responses given for the questions asked will indicate that the teacher or administrator has developed the beliefs and is demonstrating behaviors that make all students feel respected and valued.

Answer "yes" or "no" to each item. If you answer "yes" to an item, give specific examples to support your response.

1. Do I see the need to focus on the issues of groups of students who are experiencing difficulties, that is, African American males?
2. Am I open to participating in the process to develop more culturally responsive and responsible behaviors?
3. Am I willing to learn more about the culture of African American students?
4. Do I practice cultural etiquette as it relates to African American students?
5. Am I comfortable discussing issues related to race, culture, and social class?
6. Am I effective in dealing with issues related to race, culture, and social class?
7. Do I monitor my own behavior to be sure that I am not reacting on the basis of unconscious stereotyping?
8. Do I work to establish rapport and build effective relationships with African American students?
9. Have I set a goal for reducing disciplinary referrals involving African American students?
10. Do I understand my own power issues and find win–win ways to gain the respect of students?
11. Have I overcome my fear of African American males?
12. Do I seek the advice of other colleagues when I am experiencing difficulty with a particular student?
13. Do I seek to understand the motivation for student misbehavior?
14. When I have persistent conflict with a student, do I:

    a. seek to dialogue with the student?
    b. examine my own beliefs and behaviors?
    c. take seriously any comment made by the student about feeling that he is the victim of racism or prejudice, and seek to discover why he feels this way?

15. Do I allow students who have misbehaved to "start anew"?

16. Do I seek input from students regarding classroom rules and issues related to discipline?
17. Do I, to the best of my ability, try to see the world through the "eyes of my students"?
18. Have I made a commitment to be more effective in relating to and communicating with African American students?
19. Do I handle nonserious disciplinary issues in my classroom?
20. Do I examine the "precipitating factors" when an incident occurs?
21. Am I aware of my beliefs and behaviors that cause an incident to escalate?
22. Am I aware of my beliefs and behaviors that facilitate establishing good relationships with African American male students?
23. Am I aware of my beliefs and behaviors that hinder my establishing good relationships with African American students?
24. Do I "see and respect" color (i.e., differences)?
25. Do I seek to dialogue with parents about student misbehavior before it reaches a serious level?
26. Am I willing to engage in conflict resolution with a student?
27. Do I always conduct myself in a professional and ethical manner with students?
28. Do I take advantage of teachable moments to help students understand why certain behavior is inappropriate?
29. Do I engage in an ongoing process of reflection and self-assessment?
30. Have I found the Reflective Discipline model to assist me in becoming a more powerful teacher for all students?

The climate and individual assessments were designed to serve as an indicator of the extent to which new belief systems and modes of behavior are being instituted in the school environment. They provide a measure of the type of changes that individual teachers and administrators are making as well as the impact these changes have on the total school culture.

## CONCLUSION

Culturally responsive actions are those that ensure students will not receive disparate treatment as a result of conscious or unconscious bias or prejudices. In this instance, culturally responsive actions are those taken to prevent African American students from being the victims of historical myths and stereotypes. This change is based on the recognition that stereotypical images of African American males and females are both persistent and pervasive. They are also perpetuated through a cultural-conditioning process from which teachers are not immune.

Racism is a sensitive issue that many teachers and administrators find difficult to acknowledge and talk about. The mere mention of the word "race" often brings about immediate denials, defensiveness, and the "I am the exception syndrome," or "I don't see color," where individuals seek to prove that they remain untouched by the cultural-conditioning process.

At the institutional or school climate level, changes that relate to cultural responsiveness involve professional development and modifications in school practices so prejudice and discrimination of any sort do not exist in the school environment. Changes related to cultural responsiveness include a system of teacher accountability and evaluation that emphasizes the teacher's ability to demonstrate culturally sensitive behaviors toward all students.

At the individual level, cultural responsiveness involves the practice of cultural etiquette or social forms that respect the preferences and taboos of cultural groups. Changes related to cultural responsiveness will involve cognitive restructuring, a process of modifying beliefs that are based on historical myths and stereotypes.

It is imperative that we give our attention to what is happening to African American students. The disciplinary process as it is currently implemented has almost predictable outcomes, all of which are negative and especially place young African American males and females at risk for negative consequences in the larger society (Mendez 2003; Mendez and Knoff 2003). We know that:

- Suspension does not decrease inappropriate behavior; students report that being suspended did nothing to change their behavior when they felt they were unfairly suspended; it only increased their anger and potential for "defiant" behavior.
- Suspension is not a deterrent to either suspended or nonsuspended students; students see other students suspended daily and participate in the same types of behavior.
- Suspension is pervasive. For African American males, suspension begins in elementary school and continues through high school;

when asked about "the first time you remember getting into trouble," most responded that the first incident for which they were suspended occurred in elementary or middle school.

- Suspension leads to repeated suspensions; self-reports indicate that more than 50 percent of students interviewed had been suspended repeatedly.
- Suspension is negatively related to academic achievement; students interviewed reported falling behind in classes after the first three-to five-day suspension and getting failing grades with each subsequent suspension.
- Suspension leads to academic failure and dropping out of school.
- Suspension is more likely to influence a student's engagement with the criminal justice system.

Perhaps it is time that we examine the issues again and try some new approaches. Reflective Discipline is another way to view the problem. Behavioral and other change programs to change student behavior have been found to decrease school suspensions in general, but they do not eliminate racial disparity in discipline. The core issues that are the root causes of racial disparity in discipline remain unconfronted, unchallenged, and unchanged.

So where does that leave us as educators? First, we must acknowledge that race, culture, and group membership to a very large extent determine who gets referred for disciplinary actions. Second, we must recognize that exclusionary discipline works against all of our best intentions to adequately educate those most at risk for noncompletion. Finally, we must do all within our power to examine and change those things within the school setting itself which contribute to disparity in discipline.

We have spent more money and time imaginable trying to "fix students" and their parents while ignoring the fact that our schools are microcosms of the larger society and that the culturally conditioned beliefs or images that pervade the US mind are also present in our schools. It is time to honestly face ourselves, to make some fundamental changes, and to make our schools places of emotional as well as physical safety. No student should be the victim of the harm that results from the stigma imposed by historical images or ignorance of his or her culture.

Go to part V and complete reflective exercise 14.1.

# FIFTEEN
## Seeing with New Eyes

The promise of *Brown*, made more than sixty years ago, can never be achieved until each administrator, teacher, staff member, and SRO views African American and other students of color through a different lens.

There are societal and structural injustices that the individual may not have the power to correct (i.e., housing, health care, employment discrimination, and the underfunding of schools in predominately poor neighborhoods of color). But you, the "professional" in whatever role you may play are responsible for eliminating all culturally conditioned beliefs and images that blur your vision regarding the stereotypical intellectual, cultural, or moral inferiority of the black and Hispanic/Latino child who stands before you.

This book is not offered as a simple or quick solution. But it is a solution, one that requires a process of individual reflection—acknowledging, confronting, challenging, changing old belief systems, images, and ways of seeing and relating to African American and other students of color.

Change must begin in the institution to which students of color are legally forced to go each day. The central institution in the lives of black and Hispanic/Latino children must first rid itself of all the vestiges of historical, Jim Crow, and "postracial" era racism. Discrimination in our schools has a profound and lasting impact on children. In the postracial era, responsibility for racism has been shifted to the children themselves through the process of adultification. Children who have internalized this racism feel powerless, angry, and have succumbed to the belief that "this is the way I am supposed to act."

Before writing the referral, always ask:

- Who do I see standing before me?
- What is the truth of my perception?
- Is this normative behavior, behavior influenced by the School Powerlessness Syndrome, or morally inferior behavior influenced by racialized beliefs and images?

This book is focused on the African American adolescent; however, it is the reports of suspensions and arrests of African American students as early as kindergarten that is alarming. Therefore, the Reflective Discipline process is essential for all educators in K–12. The youngest of African American students deserve to begin their schooling in environments free of the influences of ill-conceived, prejudiced, and culturally conditioned beliefs and images.

Eliminating racial disparity in discipline and education inequity begins with the individual adults in charge. This book has been consistent and persistent in advocating for the role of individual responsibility in eradicating racism in our schools. As educators, we have a moral, ethical, and professional obligation to the children who enter our doors to see them with a new set of eyes. Collectively, you have the power and the control to eliminate racism in our schools.

> When teachers are free of culturally conditioned beliefs, they can create safe spaces where at the earliest ages, children can unlearn error beliefs about race. Teachers have the power and are the key to eliminating racism in American society.

# Part V

# "Reflexive" Exercises

# Appendixes

The appendices are designed to bring you to dynamic understanding of your beliefs and feelings about race and African American students in particular. All written comments are private. Therefore, please be as open and forthright as you can be. This process will free you from beliefs and images that prevent you from fully using your power as a teacher or administrator.

## APPENDIX A: COMFORT SCALE

Respond to the items based on your perceived or actual level of comfort by circling "H" for high, "M" for moderate, and "L" or low.

Be as open and honest as possible; only you will see this assessment.

1. Working in a school in which the majority of students are African American, Hispanic/Latino, American Indian, or poor.
   H M L
2. Working in a school in which the majority of students are white.
   H M L
3. Having a majority of African American males in my classroom.
   H M L
4. Being alone with a group of African American males.
   H M L
5. Working in a school in a poor neighborhood.
   H M L
6. Working in a school in a white middle- or upper-class neighborhood.
   H M L
7. Meeting with members of the African American community to discuss issues related to racial disparity in discipline.
   H M L
8. Talking about issues related to race.

H M L

9. Completing this assessment.

H M L

10. Confronting my own prejudices.

H M L

## APPENDIX B

*Beliefs Survey: Talking about Race*

Indicate the extent that you agree or disagree with the statements using the following scale:

**SA=Strongly Agree, A=Agree, D=Disagree, SD=Strongly Disagree**

1. _____ The best way to eliminate racism is to stop talking about it.

2. _____ Racism does not exist in this school.

3. _____ Teachers do not see color; all students are the same.

4. _____ I do not see a student's color when I write a referral.

5. _____ Disparity in discipline is a sign of excessive student misbehavior rather than racism.

6. _____ Disparity in discipline exists because of poverty and the culture of poverty.

7. _____ African American students misbehave more than other students.

8. _____ The punishments that African American students receive fit the magnitude of the offense.

9. _____ Racism must be eliminated in the total society before it can be eliminated in schools.

10. _____ Talking about race and racism makes me anxious.

## APPENDIX C

*Beliefs Survey: Black Boys*

Indicate the extent that you agree or disagree with the statements using the following scale:

**SA=Strongly Agree, A=Agree, D=Disagree, SD=Strongly Disagree**

_____ 1. Black boys are hostile to authority.

_____ 2. Black boys are threatening.

_____ 3. Black boys are more likely than boys from other groups to commit a violent act at school.

_____ 4. Black boys are more likely than boys from other groups to be involved in criminal activities.

_____ 5. Black boys use and sell more drugs in the school setting than boys from other groups.

_____ 6. Black boys are not interested in getting an education.

_____ 7. Black boys have no respect for females.

_____ 8. Black boys are hypersexual.

_____ 9. Black boys misbehave because they come from single-parent homes.

_____ 10. Black boys lack positive role models.

_____ 11. Black boys must be controlled in the school setting.

_____ 12 Black boys tend not to correct their behavior over time.

## APPENDIX D

*Belief Survey: Black Girls*

Indicate the extent that you agree or disagree with the statements below using the following scale:

**SA=Strongly Agree, A=Agree, D=Disagree, SD=Strongly Disagree**

_____ 1. Black girls are angry.

_____ 2. Black girls are aggressive.

_____ 3. Black girls wear suggestive clothes.

_____ 4. Black girls wear inappropriate hairstyles.

_____ 5. Black girls are highly sexual.

_____ 6. Black girls are loud.

_____ 7. Black girls are often unruly or overbearing.

_____ 8. Black girls are unladylike.

_____ 9. Black girls are domineering or bossy.

_____ 10. Black girls are more interested in boys than getting an education.

_____ 11. Black girls are often intimidating.

_____ 12. Black girls tend not to correct their behavior over time.

## CHAPTER 1: RACIAL DISPARITY IN DISCIPLINE: A PERSISTENT AND WORSENING PROBLEM

### 1.1 Discipline Research

- What are your reactions to the current research regarding racial disparity in discipline?
- Do any of your thoughts about the cause(s) of racial disparity in discipline differ from those found in research studies? If so, which ones?
- Examine discipline data for your school. What type of disparities do you find? Who receives the most referrals? For what type of offenses do these students receive referrals?
- Why do you believe the discipline statistics of your school appear this way? What do these statistics indicate to you?

### 1.2 My Referrals

This exercise is to start you thinking about the referrals that you make and the referral process.

Directions: Please read and answer honestly. No one will see this but you.

Question Yes/No

1. Have you had an excessive number of discipline referrals in the past? _____

2. Do you tend to repeatedly write referrals for a particular student?

_____

3. Do you give students the opportunity to start anew each day?

_____

4. Do you have your classroom rules posted and stated clearly?

_____

5. Do you use the services of the school counselor? _____

6. Do you use the suggestions of the school counselor once you have referred a student? _____

7. Do you show your students respect? _____

8. Is your classroom structured to ensure that students are actively engaged in learning? _____

9. Do you encourage student interaction among diverse cultural groups (e.g., seating arrangements and cooperative groups)? _____

11. Do you set high expectations for *all* students? _____

12. Do you discuss former students with other teachers in a negative way? _____

13. Do you have any preconceived notions about a particular group of students? _____

14. Do you hold grudges against students? _____

1. If you answered "yes" to items 1 and 2, what beliefs or feelings do you think are the reason?

2. Hold an image of the students for whom you repeatedly write referrals.

3. Write all of the words that come to mind about that student.

4. Do any of these words match your responses on the Beliefs Surveys B and C?

5. If you responded "yes" to talking to other teachers about students, are your discussions gossip or help sessions? What makes the difference?

6. If you responded "yes" to showing students respect, describe the ways in which you show respect to students.

7. How do you feel after you have written a referral?

Types of Referrals

For which category of offenses do you write the most referrals?

- Class disruption
- Disrespect
- Insubordination
- Defiance
- Profane language
- Tardiness
- Skipping class
- Others (e.g., horseplay, affray, etc.)

## CHAPTER 2: PERSISTENT FACTORS ESCALATING RACIAL DISPARITY IN DISCIPLINE

*2.1 Zero Tolerance*

What are your thoughts about what misbehavior should be considered zero tolerance?

_____

_____

_____

_____

_____

Have you ever referred a student for a zero-tolerance offense? If so, what was the offense? What beliefs and feelings about the event made you believe it deserved to be a zero-tolerance offense?

_____

_____

_____

_____

_____

Have you ever written referrals for misbehavior during times of high-stakes testing? If so, what beliefs and feelings about the event made you believe the student(s) should be removed from the classroom?

_____

_____

_____

_____

_____

## CHAPTER 3: NEW THREATS

The referral begins with the beliefs, thoughts, and feelings of the referral agent.

### 3.1 My Misconduct Lens

Through what lens do I view black adolescent students, as exhibiting normal behavior changes for adolescents or as willful offenders?

- Do stereotypical beliefs and images I may hold blur what is normal adolescent behavior in black adolescents?
- How does it feel at an instinctual level when a black student contradicts me? Disagrees with me? Challenges me?

- Imagine this same behavior coming from a white student? How do my beliefs, thoughts, and feelings differ?

*3.2 SRO Referrals*

Have I ever referred a black student to the SRO? For what misbehavior? Did I seek advice from the administration before referring the student? What actions taken by the student made me believe that it was a criminal rather than school disciplinary offense?

## CHAPTER 4: REFLECTIVE DISCIPLINE

The Reflective Discipline process requires that we talk about the uncomfortable subject of race and how culturally conditioned beliefs and images based on racist ideology impact relationships and behaviors in the classroom.

What are your initial thoughts about the Reflective Discipline process?

I feel _____

_____

I believe _____

_____

I learned _____

_____

I will _____

_____

## CHAPTER 5: CULTURALLY CONDITIONED BELIEFS

*The Cognitive Restructuring Process*

As you complete the exercises in this section, it is important to remember that its intent is not teacher or administrator bashing; it is rather to enhance both personal and professional empowerment. Keep these three thoughts in mind: *It is not my fault. I am the victim of a cultural conditioning process that promoted the learning of stereotypes; I can change my knowledge base and belief system; and it is my ethical responsibility to change (as a professional educator).*

Cognitive restructuring is the modification, changing, or restructuring of one's beliefs. A belief is what we perceive to be true and is a learned cognitive pattern. When a belief is erroneous, it can be unlearned to produce a newer, more accurate, and effective cognitive pattern. As more accurate cognitions replace the faulty or erroneous ones, changes in behavior will occur. Therefore, as old beliefs based on myths and stereotypes are replaced by a new set of beliefs, more culturally responsible behaviors will be developed.

Awareness is the key to becoming more culturally responsible in our interactions with African American students. Ultimately, we must experience a culturally relevant insight (CRI). A CRI results when some event occurs that enables or forces us to deal at the conscious level with some previously unconscious belief. Sometimes, we gain these insights through attending a workshop; at other times, we are forced to confront our beliefs when we work with or become friends with someone about whom we previously held stereotypical beliefs.

*5.1 Messages*

1. What is your racial, ethnic, or cultural background? How do you self-identify?

2. How old were you and how did you discover that there were racial differences?

3. What did you learn about the meaning of being white? What does it mean to be white?

4. What messages did your parents communicate to you about being white?

5. What messages did you receive from authority figures and your textbooks about the meaning of being white?

6. What messages did you receive from the larger society, the media, movies, and so on about the meaning of being white? How much does the media inform your beliefs about African Americans, especially males?

7. What messages did you receive from all sources about African Americans?

8. What beliefs and images about African Americans do you hold as a result of these messages?

9. Which of these beliefs and images do you believe are most difficult for you to release?

10. Which of these beliefs and images do you believe come into play in the classroom, especially in a conflict or discipline situation?

## CHAPTER 6: THE IMPACT OF CULTURALLY CONDITIONED BELIEFS AND IMAGES

### 6.1 Unconscious Stereotyping

For each of the following stereotypes, list specific behaviors or actions that would indicate that a teacher possibly holds beliefs about African American students, male or female, based on the stereotype. For example, if a teacher unconsciously believed that African American males were dishonest, he or she might automatically assume that when something in the classroom was missing, it was taken by an African American male. A teacher who held the beliefs that African Americans were both intellectually inferior and dishonest might insist that an African American female student cheated when she made a good grade on a test.

Culturally Conditioned Stereotypes

- Dishonest
- Aggressive/Violent
- Lazy
- Sexually Promiscuous
- Irresponsible
- Intellectually Inferior
- Dysfunctional Family

- Culturally Deprived
- Athletic
- Gang Member

Ask yourself if, in any circumstances, you have demonstrated any of those behaviors or actions.

Which of those behaviors or actions would or have students or parents felt that you demonstrated?

You might devise an anonymous method for your students to give you input regarding behaviors associated with each of the stereotypes.

Finally, monitor your behaviors and actions. If the types of actions and behaviors you have listed occur, then spend some time reflecting on the possibly unconscious beliefs that you may hold about African American students.

*6.2 Black Codes*

Monitor your reactions to African American male students, especially when they are in groups (i.e., walking down the corridor or sitting together in the cafeteria). When you feel a sense of fear, anger, or any discomfort, immediately ask yourself:

1. What am I thinking at this moment?

2. Is this thought related to a belief that I hold about African American males? What is the belief?

3. Is the belief connected to a myth or stereotype?

4. How does this thought influence my feelings and actions?

*6.3 Reflection*

When time permits, again reflect on the thoughts and feelings you experienced. Ask yourself:

- Can I honestly attribute the trait that made me feel uncomfortable to all African American male students? Why or why not?
- If all African American males are not the same, how can I change my beliefs and thoughts so that they are more objective and reflective of reality?
- Practice identifying and refuting the erroneous beliefs when your feelings and actions indicate that they are operating at an unconscious level.

## CHAPTER 7: AFRICAN AMERICAN CULTURAL PATTERNS: CULTURAL CONFLICTS AND DISCIPLINARY PRACTICES

### 7.1 African American Female Students

1. What is the nature of the conflicts that I have with African American females?
2. Which of their behaviors are most irritating to me?
3. What types of referrals do I most often write for African American females?
4. What can I do to promote better relationships with African American females?

## CHAPTER 8: COMMUNICATION CONFLICTS

### 8.1 Cultural Communication Codes

Do I believe that African Americans have a legitimate culture? Why or why not?

### 8.2 Cultural Communication Codes

Have I violated any of the communication codes in communicating with African American students? If so, which ones?

### 8.3 Cultural Communication Codes

What feelings do African American communication codes invoke in me? Why so?

### 8.4 Cultural Communication Codes

Observe your feelings and behaviors when interacting with African American students.

- Determine what you can do to ease any tension that exists between you and African students, especially males.
- Determine how you can prevent discipline events from escalating.

## CHAPTER 9: ADOLESCENT DEVELOPMENT

*9.1 Replace the Face*

Culturally conditioned beliefs and images blur our vision and prevent us from seeing normative adolescent behavior in African American students as a result of adultification. Another activity that you can use to increase your ability to experience CRIs is to "replace the face."

When you feel annoyed, angered, or uncomfortable with the manner or actions of an African American student, visualize him or her with another face.

- Then ask yourself, "How would I respond if he or she were: not African American?
- Would I see this behavior as the normal annoying behavior of an adolescent?
- Monitor your reactions to the mannerisms and actions of students who are not African American. In what ways do you react to these students differently? Why?

*9.2 Growing Up African American*

When I think of the additional developmental tasks faced by African American adolescents:

I feel _____

_____

I believe _____

_____

I learned _____

_____

I will _____

_____

## CHAPTER 10: SCHOOL DISCIPLINE AND SCHOOL CLIMATE

*10.1 The Racial Climate in Your School*

Rate the racial climate of your school in general. A 10 is a safe and supportive environment for African American students; a 1 is a hostile environment for African American students.

10......9.........8.........7.........6.........5.........4.........3.........2.........1
Safe                                                                    Hostile

- Using the same scale, how do you believe African American students would rate the racial climate of your school?
- On a scale of 10 to 1, how would you rate relationship among teachers, staff, administrators, and African American students at your school?

10......9.........8.........7.........6.........5.........4.........3.........2.........1
Supportive                                                              Distant
Caring                                                                  Nonexistent

*10.2 The School Disempowerment Syndrome*

- Have you noticed the symptoms of the School Powerlessness Syndrome among black students (i.e., anger, aggression [fights], depression, lack of esteem, loss of interest in school, excessive absentees, etc.) in your class or school in general?
- What particular symptoms have you noticed in your class?
- What symptoms do you see among black students in the school environment?
- What are your reactions to the experience of this sense of disempowerment by black students?
- Are you comfortable having a critical conversation about these feelings with the students in your classes?

*10.3 African American Reactions to School Environments*

Some of the feelings expressed by African American students in self-reports follow. Indicate the extent that you agree or disagree with the statements in relation to your school using the following scale:

**SA=Strongly Agree, A=Agree, D=Disagree, SD=Strongly Disagree**

_____ I feel disrespected.

_____ I feel like I am always being watched.

_____ I feel like I cannot speak my mind.

_____ I am perceived as being a potential thug or criminal.

_____ I am ignored until I act out.

_____ I do not feel connected here.

_____ I do not feel safe here.

_____ I do not feel supported.

_____ I do not feel like I am expected to succeed academically.

_____ I do not have a caring relationship with an adult.

*10.4 Changing the School Climate*

- How might you as an individual help to change these perceptions if they exist in your school?
- How might the faculty, staff, and administration help change negative perceptions of students in your school?
- Would you be willing to let students take a survey of their perceptions of experiences in your classroom and the school environment without fear of retribution? Why or why not?
- Are you willing to have a critical conversations in your class in relation to the survey? Why or why not?

## CHAPTER 11: THE DISCIPLINARY EVENT ANALYSIS

### 11.1 My Referrals

You have been given a model for analyzing the discipline event. Review your referrals for the last quarter or semester. For each referral answer the following questions:

- What was the perceived infraction?
- When did the perceived infraction occur?
- Who committed the perceived infraction?
- Why did the perceived infraction occur?
- How is the best way to make this a teachable moment for the student perceived to have committed the infraction?
- Was a referral as a discipline problem necessary?
- To what other possible sources could I have referred the student?
- Did classroom management influence the student's misbehavior?

### 11.2 Does This Referral Meet Criteria?

Before you write your next referral, ask and answer the questions posed in Exercise 11.1.

Become familiar with the questions; let them become second nature — internalize them. The awareness and knowledge deemed from these questions will enable you to make the best decisions regarding student misbehavior.

## CHAPTER 12: REFLECTIVE DISCIPLINE

### 12.1 Buy in

1. Am I open to the Reflective Discipline process? Why or why not?
2. Do I feel comfortable that the process focuses on individual teachers rather than students? What makes me comfortable or uncomfortable?
3. Am I ready to share my responses and insights in a group setting? Why or why not?
4. Do I believe this process will make me a better teacher? Why or why not?

## CHAPTER 13: THE VILLAGE APPROACH

*13.1 Review Appendix A: The Comfort Scale*

1. How comfortable am I in discussing issues of race with African American parents? What might give me pause?
2. Am I willing to say that I am involved in a process so that I can better teach African American students? Why or why not?
3. Do I believe that this collaboration with parents and community members can work? Decrease discipline problems? Why or why not?
4. What am I willing to do to have better communication with parents and the community?

## CHAPTER 14: EVALUATING THE PROCESS

*14.1 Evaluation of the Reflective Discipline Process*

Review the premises and tasks involved in the Reflective Discipline process.

What awareness have I gained through the process?

_____

_____

_____

_____

_____

What knowledge have I gained from the process?

_____

_____

_____

_____

_____

What skills have I learned as a result of the process?

_____

_____

_____

_____

_____

What tools or methods will I use to do a personal evaluation of my implementation of the process (e.g., number of referrals, climate of class-room, use of developmentally appropriate consequences, etc.)?

_____

_____

_____

_____

_____

## CHAPTER 15: SEEING WITH NEW EYES

*15.1 Factors Influencing Teacher Perceptions of Students*

According to Kuykendall (1992), several factors can influence the way that teachers perceive and react to students. These are a student's name, gender, socioeconomic status, previous academic record (and records of siblings), previous conduct record (and records of siblings), and appearance.

Poor African American males and females are placed in triple jeopardy of being the victim of negative perceptions, low expectations, and poor relationships with teachers as a result of stereotypical beliefs about race, gender, and poverty.

Often when a student has a name like Jerome or Jamal, a not-so-good academic record, a few previous conflicts with a teacher, and he is tall and dark in complexion, he is at a real risk of receiving a disciplinary referral and subsequent punishment. DeChanta may be flashy in her apparel and speaks her mind often. She is at risk of being judged as having low morals and being aggressive; she will most likely get referrals for dress-code violations and being disruptive and disrespectful.

Take some time to reflect on the characteristics or profiles that cause you the most difficulty in establishing rapport or communicating effectively with African American male and female students.

These exercises were designed to help you engage in a process that will make it easier to confront, challenge, and change erroneous beliefs so that you have the power to demonstrate more culturally responsive behaviors toward African American students.

# Bibliography

Advancement Project and Civil Rights Project. "Opportunities Suspended: The Devastating Consequences of Zero Tolerance and School Discipline." Washington, DC: Advancement Project; Cambridge, MA: Harvard University, Civil Rights Project, 2000.

Allen, A., L. M. Scott, and C. W. Lewis. "Racial Microaggressions and African American and Hispanic Students in Urban Schools: A Call for Culturally Affirming Education." *Interdisciplinary Journal of Teaching and Learning* 3 (2013): 117–29.

Allen, Q. "'They Think Minority Means Lesser Than': Black Middle-Class Sons and Fathers Resisting Microaggressions in the School." *Urban Education* 48, no. 2 (2012): 171–97.

Althen, G. *American Ways: A Guide for Foreigners in the United States.* Yarmouth, ME: Intercultural Press, 1988.

American Psychological Association Zero Tolerance Task Force. "Are Zero Tolerance Policies Effective in the Schools? An Evidentiary Review and Recommendations." *American Psychologist* 63, no. 9 (2008): 852–62.

Applied Research Center. "Facing the Consequences: An Examination of Racial Discrimination in U.S. Public Schools." *ERASE Report.* Oakland, CA: Applied Research Center, ERASE Initiative, 2000.

Atkinson, D., G. Morten, and D. Sue. *Counseling American Minorities: A Cross-Cultural Perspective,* 2nd ed. Dubuque, IA: William C. Brown, 1983.

Bireda, M. "The Mythical African American Male." *WEEA Digest.* Newton, MA: WEEA Resource Center, 2000.

Bireda, M. *Cultures in Conflict: Eliminating Racial Profiling,* 2nd ed. Lanham, MD: Rowman & Littlefield Education, 2010.

Boskin, J. "The National Jester in the Popular Culture." In *The Great Fear,* edited by Gary Nash and Richard Weiss, 165–85. New York: Holt, Rinehart, and Winston, 1970.

———. *The Rise and Demise of an American Jester.* New York: Oxford University Press, 1986.

Brittian, Aerika S. "Understanding African American Adolescents' Identity Development: A Relational Developmental Systems Perspective." *Journal of Black Psychology* 38, no. 2 (2012): 172–200.

Brown, J. A., D. J. Losen, and J. Wald. "Zero Tolerance: Unfair with Little Recourse." In *New Directions For Youth Development, Zero Tolerance: Can Suspension and Expulsion Keep Schools Safe?,* edited by R. J. Skiba and G. G. Noam, 73–100. San Francisco: Jossey Bass, 2001.

Brown, M. C., I. E. Dancy, and J. E. Davis. *Educating African American Males: Contexts for Consideration, Possibilities for Practice.* New York: Peter Lang, 2013.

Butler, J. P. "Of Kindred Minds: The Ties That Bind." In *Cultural Competence for Educators*, edited by Mario A. Orlandi, 23–54. Rockville, MD: US Department of Health and Human Services, 1992.

Cashmore, E., and E. McLaughlin, eds. *Out of Order? Policing Black People.* New York: Routledge, 1991.

Children's Defense Fund. "Children Out of School in America." Washington, DC: Children's Defense Fund of the Washington Research Report, 1975.

Clark, R., A. P. Coleman, and J. D. Novak. "Brief Report. Initial Psychometric Properties of the Everyday Discrimination Scale in Black Adolescents." *Journal of Adolescence* 27 (2004): 363–68.

Cokley, K. "The Impact of Racialized Schools and Racist (Mis)Education on African American Students' Academic Identity." In *Addressing Racism: Facilitating Cultural Competence in Mental Health and Educational Settings*, edited by M. G. Constantine and D. W. Sue, 127–44. Hoboken, NJ: Wiley, 2006.

Dancy, T. E., and M. C. Brown. *African American Males and Education: Researching the Convergence of Race and Identity.* Charlotte, NC: Information Age Publishing, 2012.

Dandy, E. B. *Black Communication: Breaking Down the Barriers.* Chicago: African American Images, 1991.

Epstein, R., J. J. Blake, and T. Gonzalez. *Girlhood Interrupted: The Erasure of Black Girls' Childhood.* Washington, DC: The Center on Poverty and Inequality, Georgetown Law, 2015.

Eyler, J., V. Cook, and L. Ward. "Resegregation: Segregation within Desegregated Schools." In *The Consequences of School Desegregation*, edited by Christine Rossell and Willis D. Hawley, 210–329. Philadelphia: Temple University Press, 1983.

Fisher, C. B., S. A. Wallace, and R. E. Fenton. "Discrimination Distress during Adolescence." *Journal of Youth and Adolescence* 29, no. 6 (2000): 679–95.

Ferguson, A. A. *Bad Boys: Public Schools in the Making of Black Masculinity.* Ann Arbor: University of Michigan Press, 2003.

Glasser, William. *Control Theory in the Classroom.* New York: Harper Row, 1986.

Goff, P. A., M. C. Jackson, B. A. L. Di Leone, M. C. Culotta, and N. DiTomasso. "The Essence of Innocence: Consequences of Dehumanizing Black Children." *Journal of Personality and Social Psychology* 106, no. 4 (2014): 526–45.

Greenfield, P. M., C. Raeff, and B. Quiroz. "Cultural Values in Learning and Education." In *Closing the Achievement Gap: A Vision for Changing Beliefs and Practices*, edited by Belinda Ho, 37–55. Arlington, VA: Association for Supervision and Curriculum Development, 1996.

Hadden, Sally E. *Slave Patrols: Law and Violence in Virginia and the Carolinas.* Harvard Historical Studies, Book 138. Cambridge, MA: Harvard University Press, 2003.

Hale-Benson, J. E. *Black Children: Their Roots, Culture, and Learning Styles.* Baltimore, MD: John Hopkins University Press, 1986.

Henfield, M. S. "Black Male Adolescents Navigating Microaggressions in a Traditionally White Middle School: A Qualitative Study." *Journal of Multicultural Counseling and Development* 39 (2011): 141–55.

Herskovits, M. J. *The Myth of the Negro Past.* Boston: Beacon Press, 1958.

Hillard, A. "Alternatives to IQ Testing: An Approach to the Identification of Gifted Minority Children." In *Black Children: Their Roots, Culture, and Learning Styles*, edited by J. E. Benson, 43. Baltimore, MD: John Hopkins University Press, 1986.

Ho, M. K. *Family Therapy with Ethnic Minorities.* Newbury, CA: Sage, 1987.

Hodgkinson, H. *Secondary Schools in a New Millennium: Demographic Certainties, Social Realities.* Reston, VA: National Association of Secondary School Principals, 2000.

Howard, T. C. *Why Race and Culture Matters in Schools: Closing the Achievement Gap in America's Classrooms.* New York: Teachers College Press, 2010.

Hyman, I. A., and P. A. Snook. *Dangerous Schools: What We Can Do about the Physical and Emotional Abuse of Our Children.* San Francisco, CA: Jossey-Bass Publishers, 1999.

Johnston, R. "Federal Data Highlight Disparities in Discipline." *Education News* (June 21, 2000.

Joint Center for Political Studies. *Visions of a Better Way: A Black Appraisal of Public Schooling.* Washington, DC: Joint Center for Political Studies Press, 1989.

Kappeler, V. E. A Brief History of Slavery as the Origin of American Policing. Retrieved from https://prisonline/edu.edu/brief-history-slavery-and-origins-american-policing

Kuykendall, C. *From Rage to Hope: Strategies for Reclaiming Black and Hispanic Students.* Bloomington, IN: National Educational Service, 1992.

Locke, D. C. *Increasing Multicultural Understanding: A Comprehensive Model.* Newbury Park, CA: Sage, 1992.

Loewenberg, P. "The Psychology of Racism." In *The Great Fear,* edited by Gary Nash and Richard Weiss, 186–201. New York: Holt, Rinehart, & Winston, 1970.

Lynch, E. W., and M. J. Hanson. *Developing Cross-Cultural Competence: A Guide for Working with Young Children and Their Families.* Baltimore, MD: Paul H. Brookes Publishing, 1992.

Mattison, E., and M. S. Abner. "Closing the Achievement Gap: The Association of Racial Climate with Achievement and Behavioral Outcomes." *American Journal of Community Psychology* 40 (2007): 1–12.

Mendez, L. M. R., and Knoff, H. M. "Who Gets Suspended from School and Why? A Demographic Analysis of Schools and Disciplinary Infractions in a Large School District." *Education and Treatment of Children* 26, no. 1 (2003): 30–51.

Mendez, L. M. R. "Predictors of Suspension and Negative School Outcomes: A Longitudinal Investigation." In *New Directions for Youth Development,* no. 99, *Deconstructing the School to-Prison Pipeline,* edited by J. Wald and D. J. Losen, 17–33. San Francisco: Jossey Bass, 2003.

Meirer, K., J. Stewart, and R. England. *Race, Class, and Education: The Politics of Second-Generation Discrimination.* Madison: University of Wisconsin Press, 1989.

Morris, Monique. *Pushout: The Criminalization of Black Girls in Schools.* New York: New Press, 2016.

Newby, I. A. *Jim Crow's Defense: Anti-Negro Thought in America 1900–1930.* Baton Rouge: Louisiana State University, 1965.

Office of Civil Rights. *Student Discipline.* Washington, DC: HEW Fact Sheet, 1974.

———. *Racial Incidents and Harassment against Students at Educational Institutional Guidance,* no. 59. Washington, DC: Federal Register 11448, 10 March 1994.

———. *Proactive Docket Activities—Fiscal Year 2001.* Atlanta, GA: Southern Division, 2001.

———. Annual Report to Congress (2001–2002). Part 3: Strategic Priorities. Retrieved on June 17, 2009, from: http:/www.ed.gov/about/offices/list/ocr/AnnRpt2002/edlite-2002arc-3html

Noguera, P. *The Trouble with Black Boys and Other Reflections on Race, Equity, and the Future of Public Education.* San Francisco: Wiley & Sons, 2003.

Oliver, W. "Reflections on Manhood." In *Images of Color: Images of Crime*, edited by Coramae Mann and Marjorie Zatz, 81. Los Angeles: Roxbury, 1998.

Omusu-Bempah, Akwasi. "Race and Policing in Historical Context: Dehumanization and the Policing of Black People in the 21st Century." *Theoretical Criminology* 21, no. 1 (2017): 23–34.

Paul, A. M. "Where Bias Begins: The Truth about Stereotypes." *Psychology Today* 31 (May/June 1998): 52–56.

Peretti, P. O. "Effects of Teacher's Attitudes on Discipline Problems in Schools Recently Desegregated." In *The Consequences of School Desegregation*, edited by Christine Rossell and Willis Hawley. Philadelphia: Temple University Press, 1983.

Polite, V. C., and J. E. Davis. *African American Males in School and Society: Practices and Policies for Effective Education*. New York: Teachers College Press, 1999.

Rausch, M. K., and Skiba, R. J. *The Academic Cost of Discipline: The Relationship between Suspension/Expulsion and School Achievement*. Retrieved February 5, 2008, from http://www.agi.harvard.edu/Search/download.php?id=45

Reddick, L. D. "The Nineteen Basic Stereotypes of Blacks in American Society." *Journal of Negro Education* 12 (1944).

Rome, D. "Stereotyping by the Media: Murderers, Rapists, and Drug Addicts." In *Images of Color: Images of Crime*, edited by Coramae Mann and Marjorie Zatz, 86–87. Los Angeles: Roxbury, 1998.

Scott, L. D. "The Relation of Racial Identity and Racial Socialization to Coping with Discrimination among African American Adolescents." *Journal of Black Studies* 33 (2003): 520–38.

Sellers, R. M., N. Copeland-Linder, P. P. Martin, and R. L. Lewis. "Racial Identity Matters: The Relationship between Racial Discrimination and Psychological Function in African American Adolescents." *Journal of Research on Adolescence* 16, no. 2 (2006): 187–216.

Skiba, R. J., M. Arredondo, C. Gray, and M. K. Rausch. "What Do We Know about Discipline Disparities? New and Emerging Research." In *Inequality in School Discipline*, edited by R. J. Skiba, K. Mediratta, and M. K. Rausch, eds. Bloomington: University of Indiana, The Equity Project, 2016.

Skiba, R. J., and Knesting, K. "Zero Tolerance, Zero Evidence: An Analysis of School Disciplinary Practice." In *New Direction for Youth Development, Zero Tolerance: Can Suspension and Expulsion Keep Schools Safe?*, edited by R. J. Skiba and G. G. Noam, 17–44. San Francisco: Jossey Bass, 2001.

Skiba, R. J., R. S. Michael, A. C. Nardo, and Peterson, R. *The Color of Discipline: Sources of Racial Gender Disproportionality in School Punishment*. Bloomington: University of Indiana Education Policy Center, 2000.

Spencer, M. B., M. Cunningham, and D. P. Swanson. "Identity as Coping: Adolescent African-American Males' Adaptive Responses to High-Risk Environments." In *Racial and Ethnic Identity: Psychological Development and Creative Expression*, edited by H. W. Harris, H. C. Blue, and E. E. H. Griffiths, eds., 31–52. New York: Routledge, 1995.

Sobel, M. *The World They Made Together: Black and White Values in Eighteenth-Century Virginia*. Princeton, NJ: Princeton University Press, 1987.

Sue, D. W., A. I. Lin, G. C. Torino, C. M. Capodilupo, and D. P. Rivera. Racial Microaggressions and Difficult Dialogues on Race in the Classroom. *Cultural Diversity and Ethnic Minority Psychology* 15, no. 2 (2009): 183–90.

Tatum, B. D. *Why Are All the Black Kids Sitting Together in the Cafeteria?* New York: Basic Books, 1997.

US Department of Education. *Civil Rights Data Collection for the 2015–2016 School Year.* Washington, DC: The Office of Civil Rights, 2018.

Wallace, J. M., S. Goodkind, C. M. Wallace, and J. G. Bachman. "Racial, Ethnic, and Gender Differences in School Discipline among U.S. High School Students: 1991–2005." *Negro Educational Review* 59, no. 1–2 (2008): 47–62.

Wald, J., and D. Losen. "Defining and Redirecting a School-to-Prison Pipeline." In *New Directions for Youth Development*, no. 99, *Deconstructing the School-to-Prison Pipeline*, edited by J. Wald and D. J. Losen, 9–15. San Francisco: Jossey-Bass, 2003.

Willis, W. "Families with African American Roots." In *Developing Cross-Cultural Competence: A Guide for Working with Young Children and Their Families*, edited by E. W. Lynch and M. J. Hanson. Baltimore, MD: Paul H. Brookes, 1992.

Witt, H. "School Discipline Harder on Blacks: Analysis of Federal Data Shows Racial Inequity in Suspensions and Expulsions Nationwide; Locally the Gap Is Widest in Lake and Dupage." *Chicago Tribune*. Retrieved June 18, 2009, from http://archives.chicagotribune.com/2007/sep/25/news/discipline

Wong, C. A., J. S. Eccles, and A. Sameroff. "The Influence of Ethnic Discrimination and Ethnic Identification on African American Adolescents' School and Socioemotional Adjustment." *Journal of Personality* 71 (2003): 1197–1232.

Wynn, C. "Black and White Bibb County Classrooms." In *The Consequences of School Desegregation*, edited by Christine Rossell and Willis Hawley, 145. Philadelphia: Temple University Press, 1983.

# Workshops

Dr. Bireda presents keynote addresses and facilitates workshops for administrators, teachers, and parents related to the practice of Reflective Discipline.

If you would like to receive information about keynote addresses or workshops, please contact:

The Bireda Group
P.O. Box 510818
Punta Gorda, Florida 33951
(941) 639-2914
Email: biredagrp5@yahoo.com

# About the Author

**Martha R. Bireda**, PhD, has more than twenty-five years' experience as a consultant and trainer specializing in issues related to race and ethnicity, gender, cultural diversity, and socioeconomic class. She is a frequent keynote speaker, instructor, and facilitator of dialogues related to race and cultural diversity. Dr. Bireda provides training and consultation related to eliminating racial disparity in discipline to school districts.

In addition, Dr. Bireda facilitates cultural sensitivity training for law enforcement. She served as a subject-matter specialist and trainer for the Human Diversity curriculum developed by the Florida Department of Law Enforcement and the Florida Department of Corrections. Most recently, Dr. Bireda was a member of the advisory group appointed by the Florida Department of Law Enforcement Criminal Justice Standards and Training Commission to assist commission initiatives to strengthen the relationship between law enforcement and the community.

Dr. Bireda serves on the advisory board for the Institute for Intergovernmental Research, which facilitates the VALOR Initiative sponsored by the US Department of Justice, Bureau of Justice Assistance.

Dr. Bireda has authored articles "Education for All" (2000) and "The Mythical African American Male" (2000). She published several editions of *Cultures in Conflict: Eliminating Racial Profiling* (2002, 2010). In 2011, Dr. Bireda published *Schooling Poor Minority Children: New Segregation in the Post-Brown Era* (2011).

She also writes a monthly column in *Wall Street International Magazine* in the Economy and Politics section and can be found under Dr. Martha R. Bireda on Facebook.

Dr. Bireda is director of the Blanchard House Museum of African American History and Culture of Charlotte County and lives in Florida.